I'M IN!

JOURNEY INWARD TO DISCOVER YOUR WHO

JOHN STIX

Author's Personal Note

This book is dedicated to everyone who has been a part of my own unique journey of Discovering who I am. A very special thank you to my wife, my dad, my best friend, my pastor, my grandma, and the rest of my family who have all helped me to see me for who I truly am.

To my co-author Chrissy, I wish to thank you for your dedication to this project along with the intention of helping others.

I feel very blessed and am truly thankful for the most important aspect in my life which is my faith in Christ Jesus.

Your life's purpose is to go on a journey to discover your WHO, and release the fullest potential of you into the world.

CONTENTS

INTRODUCTION: ARE YOU IN?

I'm In™ is my company's mantra; it's our emotional bond. It represents the moment when two entrepreneurs are talking about the vision they have to build something that will change the world, and they're not talking about the fancy cars they'll one day drive or the huge shining towers they'll one day build. What they're saying is, "Do you hear the dream I'm describing? Can you see the vision? Are you IN?"

"I'm In" is also my personal mantra. It's a daily reminder to align my outward life with my authentic self by looking inward to remember who I am. This process of looking and living inward began for me back in 2013, at a time when I was feeling disengaged and out of alignment with my life. I was carrying around a heavy sense that my life was not what it should be and a guilt that I couldn't enjoy what I had worked so hard to accomplish. I felt unfulfilled. It was an effort to get out of bed every morning and go to work, and that disengagement was creeping into every area of my life, keeping me from experiencing joy. I was disconnected in my friendships and work relationships, unable to express myself, and detached from some of the people I should have been closest to. I couldn't understand why I felt so distant from the life I was living and the work I was doing. After all, I was the author of my life, so shouldn't it be everything I had ever wanted?

That same year I was looking around my workplace at the business that I had co-founded and helped to build, and I saw a company that was struggling with the same issues. Our leadership team was disjointed and passionless. Our business was besieged by infighting, unresolved issues, HR concerns, and a growth curve that was going the wrong way. The other leaders and I were unhappy and disengaged and we looked around every day at teams of people who were also unhappy and disengaged — people who were no longer finding joy and purpose in their work. We knew something had to change but had no real idea of where to start.

Through a series of deep-dive talks, we realized that we had forgotten the company's original dreams. We had forgotten why it existed, what we had initially set out to achieve, and how we'd wanted to achieve it. We had forgotten everything that made the company *who* it was. It was only by going through a process to remember the WHO of the company that we were able to remember its purpose, let go of old hurts and misunderstandings, and have everyone feel "in" again.

Knowing our WHO enabled us to make massive workplace culture changes and set our company on a new path of growth. Inside of a year we turned the company around and revealed our true company identity to the world. We experienced new growth and attracted new employees, customers, and clients who identified with our WHO.

We also ended up winning the Best Employer Branding award in 2015 from the Canadian Human Resource Association.

The results we achieved are why I get invited to speak about workplace culture and to consult with other businesses. I talk about the steps we went through and the culture changes we enacted in an effort to bring joy and purpose back to our workplace and effect incredible growth and internal engagement. I also mentor other businesses to help them discover their WHO so that they can experience similar alignment and engagement.

But more and more during these sessions, I find myself discussing the personal changes that occurred in me leading up to and going through our corporate changes. Because as we were diving into finding the WHO of the business, I embarked on a similar journey to rediscover my own WHO. It was a journey of looking and living inward to uncover my true identity and reveal my true purpose and potential in my life.

It's a way of living that I've started to share with others because I see so many business leaders, friends, employees, colleagues, and family members feeling the same way that I did:

Disconnected

Alone

Restless

Unsettled

I see them behaving as I did — frantically searching for answers outside of themselves. I was busy asking everyone I knew for advice about how to feel less stressed and less tired, and yet I couldn't stop racing from activity to activity, trying to find something to connect to, something that would make me feel engaged and purpose-filled again.

It wasn't until the morning that I physically walked away from the door of my business that I understood that the reason I was feeling disconnected and didn't know what to do, was that I didn't know who I was. I needed to stop looking for answers around me and start looking IN. Before I could know *what* to do, I had to know *who* I was.

Maybe you're experiencing this disconnection in your own life.

Maybe you have toxic relationships, anxiety, and stress.

Maybe you have a measure of success but know that the success was built upon a foundation that isn't really you.

You feel the pressure of everyone looking at your success and thinking you have it all. The very accomplishments that don't feel right and are not a reflection of you are a trap because of the pressure of having to maintain that success.

You're living a life that you know deep down isn't a reflection of you, but you're afraid to act.

There's a gap between the life you are living and who you believe yourself to be. What holds you back from jumping that gap?

Judgement from others?

Judgement from self?

Fear of loss of success?

Fear of loss of income?

Fear of loss of relationships?

Fear of loss of what you've built and your reputation?

But perhaps above all, what holds you back is the fear of never knowing your true purpose in this life, that one day you will leave this world saying, "I was never me. I never knew what I was capable of or knew my full potential."

Everyone wants to know their purpose. I look around and see everyone asking, "What book can I read? What podcast can I listen to? What test can I take that will reveal my true purpose and potential?"

I believe your purpose is the same as mine. We all have the same purpose:

> It is to discover who you really are.
>
> It is to unhook yourself from what holds you back and then unleash the truest expression of yourself to the world.

It is only by looking inward to discover your WHO that you will find a life where you are able to live out the dreams of your heart — a life that is a direct reflection of who you are. Only by knowing your WHO can you experience a life of true purpose.

Living inward enabled me to realize the dreams I have for my life and to know how to bring them to fruition, let go of pain from the past, and experience true joy and contentment in my life.

By uncovering my identity, I discovered a true love for myself and others and a desire to see everyone find their own WHO and live it. To put on their cape and be their own super hero. To love themselves enough to chase the dreams that are firmly rooted in who they are. My wish for you is that you will use this book to go on your own living inward journey, to discover your true purpose rooted within your identity.

I've written this book from the perspective of a business leader, because that's one aspect of who I am. I've written this book for other business leaders to show them the power of discovering the WHO of their business. The examples of how I lived out my WHO take place mostly within my workplace, because that was where I felt the most disengaged and where I see the most disengagement and dissatisfaction in other people's lives. By discovering and releasing who you really are, I believe you can find new passion and purpose in your day-to-day work.

But at the heart of it, this is not a lesson about workplace culture. It is about a personal journey I went on. Yes, it impacted my business, and yes, I believe the steps laid out in this book can be used by business leaders to impact their businesses. But the living inward journey is one that anyone can go on, and the steps and the lessons within can be applied to any area of your life. Whether you're a business leader or not, you can effect change in your organization, in your family, in your relationships, in your career — in every aspect of your life — just by knowing your WHO.

You can use this book to help you on your own living inward journey. Start with one aspect of your life in which you are feeling the most disengaged, and work through the practices in this book. Then, use the lined pages at the end of each practice to take notes on what you learn about yourself, about the dreams you find deep within, about who you discover yourself to be, and about what your authentic life looks like.

I don't believe I have the answers on how to direct each individual person's life. What I'm sharing is a journey. Your journey of looking and living inward will be uniquely your own. This can make the journey seem intimidating, because no one can show you your own path. But what I know and believe most deeply in my heart is that every person deserves to know their life identity. It's your birthright. It's why you're here.

No matter how busy you are or how many people count on you, if you aren't in touch with who you are as a person, you will always be seeking — you will always have questions.

Living inward is a journey of answers, of healing, of discovery, of shedding the false self, and of shining a light of awareness on your true self and revealing that true self to others. It's about following a path to discover your WHO, to find real purpose and real fulfillment, and to once again experience joy, authentic relationships with others, and love on an unimaginable scale.

Are you IN?

STAGE I
Identity is Key

"We are to discover who we are, then release our potential to the world."

John Stix

CHAPTER 1: YOUR WHO COMES FIRST

Who Am I?

On a sunny Wednesday morning in the summer of 2013, I arrived at work, put out my hand to open the front door of the building, and pulled it back. I returned to my car, leaned back in the driver's seat, and said out loud,

"I don't want to be here."

This may not sound like an original story — we all have days when we don't want to go to work. But for me, it went deeper than that. This wasn't just my place of employment. This was the company I had co-founded with my lifelong friend almost two decades before, when we jumped into what was arguably the most competitive arena in the country. With little more than a dream of an idea scratched on a pub napkin, we took on the internet and telecommunications incumbents from a makeshift office in our basement and grew our business into one of the largest telecom companies in Canada.

In those early basement days in the late 1990s, communication and connection came easily. We sat together day and night, joined at the hip by the vision of setting our business apart from what we felt were the cumbersome, lethargic companies that owned the market share at the time.

We were nimble, buoyant, fast, and incredibly determined. I remember times when a paycheque was a bonus — times when the sense of accomplishment was literally our pay. There were significant risks to take, but the big dreams both demanded those risks and carried us through years of peaks and valleys, challenge and success.

I doubt any Human Resources department would have approved of our working environment at the time, but we managed to fill six new desks with employees as our growth dictated that we needed them. Job candidates showed up at the house with confused expressions — I'm sure some of them left as soon as they drove down the crescent and realized that our company was also our home. For those who stayed, we welcomed them with open arms and kept moving forward with a core team who stepped up to do anything they could to further the dream.

Time and again, we proved that the difference between stagnation and success was in seeing a "No" not as a wall that could stop us but simply a challenge whose solution would bring us closer to our dream. The problems stimulated, inspired, and bound us together even more tightly with a common purpose. I personally was too oblivious to the possibility of anything being a threat. It was just what we did: overcome! We didn't know the words "workplace culture" and we hadn't yet defined our mantra; our company fabric stayed happy and connected by all of us being together, and we were definitely all "IN." But as we outgrew that basement, and our team's size increased from 10 to 100 to 200, and we opened our offsite office in the Dominican Republic, it became harder and harder to keep that happy culture alive.

And now here it was, over fifteen years later, and I was sitting in my car outside the very dream that I had helped to create, and I just didn't want to be there anymore. On the other side of the front door, issues were festering. There was increased bickering and less communication, and HR complaints were on the rise. I saw leaders working in their silos, walking around holding things close to their chests, not feeling safe to share. For the first time in our company's history, our growth had dipped below 10%. If someone had assembled the entire leadership team and asked each of us for our elevator pitch, we would've all said different things. We no longer knew who the company was or how we were to communicate who we were to others.

Just a few evenings earlier, I had been sitting with a friend in one of the very pubs my co-founder and I used to sit in to talk about our dream. My friend, who is also a customer, said, "John, I have to tell you something, and it pains me to say it, but it's not a pleasure dealing with your company anymore."

I knew we had a very serious problem that had gone way beyond the leaders. A thread of disengagement had woven itself into the very fabric of our company, and if it continued, it would rip us apart. I was overwhelmed with the task ahead of me, not even sure that I had the energy to initiate the changes that were needed. Like my company, I too had issues festering inside of me, and I was increasingly unhappy. My relationships lacked authentic dialogue, and I felt out of step with those around me, incapable of communicating to the outside world who I thought I was at a fundamental level. As a leader, I was hard to approach and seen as being removed, distant, and difficult to get to know. For months, I had been tired, operating in a state of numbness and telling friends I was burned out — a term that allowed me to feel safe and to hide from them and myself the sense of complete disconnection I felt inside.

"Take a vacation, John," they'd say.

I'd go away, come home, and tell them nothing had changed.

"You must have taken the wrong vacation!" they'd say.

I received a lot of advice — all of it well intentioned — but of course none of it worked. How could it when I wasn't being honest about the real issues going on? Admittedly, at the time, I didn't even know what the real issues were.

On the outside, people saw a confident, successful business owner, but inside, I had lost my passion and sense of purpose, and in its place was growing a hopeless, empty feeling that I couldn't hide or deny any longer. For so long, my personal identity had been bound up in the identity of the company, and suddenly, sitting there in my car, I didn't know who either of them was anymore.

What's wrong with me? I'm the one who made my life the way it is, so it should be everything I want. But if I feel disengaged and out of alignment with the life and the business I created, then really, WHO AM I?

> Do you identify with the me of six years ago, sitting in my car, not really knowing who I was?
>
> Do you have the feeling that something isn't quite right in your life?

Although outwardly your life might appear to be everything you want it to be, inside there is a sense of collapse and decay. Nothing feels quite right. There's disengagement and misalignment, and there are issues that aren't being dealt with.

You feel out of step with those around you, you feel "unseen," and you feel like you're in the hamster wheel, running fast and going nowhere.

There's a lot of busyness without a sense that what's being accomplished is meaningful or purposeful. Every day is about getting up and doing what needs to be done, just to get to the next day and do it all over again.

Are you asking yourself, as I did:

> What is the point of all of this?

> What am I doing and why am I doing it?
>
> Who is this person living my life?
>
> **Who am I?**

The despair behind that last question hit me full force. What a sensation it was to realize that I didn't know who I really was, that I didn't know my true identity. I had been living an outward, action-filled life, and in asking other people for their advice about how to feel engaged and connected again, I had been looking outside myself for the answers.

Was it possible that I needed to turn inward to remember who I truly was?

And was it possible that, as a company, we had to turn inward to discover our true identity so we could move forward again?

I can tell you right now that the short answer to both of these questions was yes. When there is misalignment and disengagement, taking the time to ask, "Who am I?" is the first step of the living inward journey, because identity is the key for both businesses and individuals.

> If you don't know who you are, how can you know what to do, or even why you're doing it?
>
> If you don't know who you are, any decision you

make won't really be coming from you. You'll never feel engaged with the decision or feel that it has any meaning or purpose in your life.

Before the why, the how, or the when, your WHO must come first.

This is why I get hired to consult: to help organizations and individuals find their WHO. When the leaders discover and remember who the company is, they can clearly see where the company is capable of going and make the right decisions to get it there. But before we get into discovering the WHO of the business, I begin with several exercises to help the leadership team uncover their WHO as individuals.

This usually leads to confusion and questions: "I thought we were here to find the identity of the company. Why am I having to focus so much on myself?"

My answer comes in three parts.

First, the company is a living, breathing entity, made up of living, breathing individuals. If you don't know who the leaders are that make up the company, you will never know who the company is.

Second, as a business leader, you need to know who you are to be able to authentically lead the company. You need to know that who you are aligns with who the company is. Otherwise, you will

> never be able to successfully lead that company.
>
> And finally, you, as an individual, have the right to know who you truly are, to know what your true purpose is in this life, whether you're a leader or not.

If you aren't in touch with who you are as a person, you will always feel out of alignment. You will always be seeking, and you will always have questions.

You're not alone if you're wondering, "Who am I? What is my purpose? Why am I here?" These are big and sometimes scary questions. But seeking the answer to these questions and living out your true self are natural and instinctive. At the beginning of our lives, and often again near the end, we are truly ourselves because it's all that really matters. As babies and young children, we live out our authentic and vulnerable inner selves without self-judgement or fear of judgement from others. When we're young, we are singularly focused on the moment, knowing instinctively who we are and what we need. And as we near the end of life, we are often too weak and tired, or too wise and strong to be anyone but ourselves.

But somewhere between exploration and wisdom, we lose ourselves. We construct a false sense of self, based on what we believe we must to do survive, and we develop and wear masks that are false manifestations of ourselves. These masks cover up who we truly are, and they lead us towards actions that are also false — that are consistent with the false sense of self. This is what creates the false ego, or shadow self.

The false ego wakes up every day chasing what it wishes to have, what it prioritizes:

Money

Popularity

Attention

The list goes on.

And every day, we present that false self to the world to get what we think we need, feeding the false self with outward routines and activities that trap us, disconnecting us from our true self and reinforcing the masks over time by chasing what the masks covet.

But ask yourself this: If what you want is determined by the masks you wear, and the masks you wear are what allow you to exist in a false state, then what aspects of your life through thoughts, actions, and desires are really even you anymore?

Who or what owns your thoughts and actions?

Over the years, the buildup of masks and adaptations, through busy outward living, has fed into the lie that you have to live someone else's life, leading to this feeling of disconnection and disengagement, leading to this moment when you're looking at yourself, wondering whose life you're living. Many of your actions are necessary for you to exist in your current state, but that state and those actions are not representative of who you really are.

Your masks do not define you. Your authentic self defines you and wants to live out your real purpose. This is why the actions of your false self will never properly represent you and will never feel quite right.

Ironically, it is the buildup of the false beliefs and the false ego that provides a beautiful entry point for asking, "Who Am I?" You may have arrived at this point from any of a number of different directions. You may be hurting, torn apart by a life bomb — a moment when you're taken from everything in your life being OK to suddenly being on your knees, not knowing what hit you or how you're going to get up again, but knowing that after this moment you will never be the same. Or you're here because, while everything in your life may seem outwardly all right, inside, you're increasingly aware that it's not. You know you're in the hamster wheel and no longer want to live this way and you believe you don't have to, but you may be overwhelmed, thinking about how to get started, and fearing what will happen next.

You can shatter the limitations the false self has placed on you by simply looking inward and remembering who you are.

Sitting in my car that day, I realized that no one else is responsible for my life other than me. I accepted that I would find the answers inside, and I opened the door, literally and figuratively, with a willingness and a thirst to find out who I was.

Openness is the first principle in this early stage. Change will come later, but for now, openness is something you practise on a daily basis.

"I remain open to all possibilities in my life and I am willing to discover WHO I AM."

This is your mantra to keep you committed to living inward. Say it out loud to yourself and say it every day. It will provide you with a sense of curiosity and adventure, and a belief that change is possible, and it sets the stage for profound transformation. A commitment to openness and looking inward will reveal what's truly important to you, what truly matters to you. By remembering who you are, you will reveal your true purpose, a purpose that will remove that sense of disconnection and have you bounding out of bed in the morning, filled with joy at the thought of the day ahead.

It's time to stop looking for answers in the outward journey. The view of your authentic self becomes clear when you take the time to look inward and ask,

"Who Am I?"

PRACTICE: Who Am I?

Background

I know that life is full of incredibly fast routines in your quest to move forward and that, so often, they just lead you further away. This practice is about shifting your direction and going inward, by slowing down, being quiet, and listening.

Daily asking myself, "Who Am I?" has had such an impact on my life and circumstances that I can say I will certainly never be the same again, nor would I want to be. With just three small but incredibly powerful words, this simple practice is transformational when accompanied by a sense of wonder and curiosity. This question is the front door to a path that sets you on the journey inward to remember who you are, allowing you to let go of ego and drop the masks that you feel are demanded by yourself and others. It will unleash the very essence of you, while allowing dreams to come to the surface and be realized.

That sense of disconnection that you feel with your life means that, in the heart of you, there is a YOU that you don't even know. That sense of disconnection means that there is a phone ringing in your life and on the other end of the line is the authentic you who has a message about who you truly are. Embracing openness in this practice is about slowing down and taking time to listen to your true self and learn to be just you, once again.

Find a space and time to be alone and quiet for this practice.

The practice in Chapter 2 will be about finding a specific place for you, but for today, just find a place where you can be alone for a few minutes and be quiet. It's not strictly about having quiet all around you, but more about finding a quiet space inside of you — because you can be sitting still with no noise around you, but if your mind is ruminating and your insides are churning, you won't hear your small internal voice. The key to this practice is to slow down and embrace listening.

The Practice

In your quiet space take a few deep breaths and picture in your mind a place that makes you feel peaceful or where you find it easy to slow down your thinking. It could be a beach, or a forest, or a place from your childhood where you used to go and dream. If it helps position yourself near certain sounds, like birds or soft music. I have a deep affinity with water and have an easier time being quiet inside my head when it's raining. Find what works for you to bring you to a mindful moment of quiet.

Now, out loud, say the words, "Who Am I?"

Repeat them, putting the emphasis on different words. Say it quickly, and then slowly, and then with a pause between each word.

Keep repeating it.

And then pause.

Listen for that still, small voice, that inner voice that wants to tell you the truth.

Repeat it as many times as you need, until you're ready to write down the answers that come to you. You can use the lined pages that follow or your own journal, if you have one. You may see an image, or hear words, or just have a vague sense of an emotion. You may not see or hear anything. There may be no words yet to describe what you see. That's OK. Years of wearing masks can make it difficult to remember who you are in your most authentic form. For now, be comfortable with not knowing what this sensation is, and keep repeating the practice daily. Slowly you will gain a clearer picture of who you are inside, of who you are authentically, and you can start journalling once you have something to say.

You won't need to do anything yet with what you see. You don't need to make any changes in your life as a result of what you hear. Even if your outward life seems so far removed from what you're learning about yourself, this is a stage of listening, not doing.

Go into each day's practice with purposeful acceptance and without judgement. Let your daily mantra be, "I accept where I am in this moment. I accept who I am in this moment."

As you move through other practices in this book, continue to return daily to the question "Who Am I?" The answer you get, just like the living inward journey itself, will be intensely personal and just for you. The path you take to find the authentic you will be just as unique as the YOU who you find along the path, because you are the path and the path is you. Feel a sense of excitement about what you are going to discover and how your life is about to change.

CHAPTER 2: THE SEED OF CARE

Finding the Seed of Care

I did eventually make it out of my car and into my office that morning. I sat at my desk and thought. *Everyone around me can feel that I'm disengaged. I need to try and fix myself, and I need to try and fix my company.*

I had no idea where to start, so I did what I thought any good leader would do. I opened my laptop and Googled "Unhappy employees in the workplace... WHY??"

I spent weeks reading about empowering and nurturing teams. I reread articles about innovation that had once inspired me, but now I read the message between the lines. In an article about Steve Jobs, I saw that where I'd thought he was talking about how to be innovative, he was actually talking about how everyone in the company — from marketing, to product development, to packaging, to finance — had engaged with a dream and then pulled together to bring it to reality.

For the first time, I heard the quotation "Culture eats strategy for breakfast" and became actively engaged in figuring out what that meant.

I dove into the wisdom of ancient leaders to learn about what had empowered them to inspire others to come together and achieve great things.

I found a small spark of excitement and hope for my organization, but I was still ignoring the deeper issues within myself. My days and nights were filled with worrying about my company, and any questions I had about myself just led to more questions, with no time to look for answers.

An opportunity came up to go to Vancouver, a city that has always felt like a second home to me. I jumped at the chance of spending a few days alone, hoping that some quiet time jogging through Stanley Park and sitting by the water in English Bay would give me the freedom to listen to my own thoughts and learn why I felt so disconnected.

As the plane touched down in Vancouver, I enjoyed a familiar sense of peace, swiftly followed by a sense of adventure. At that point in my life, I was very much an "A to B" sort of guy, always with a goal in mind before I set off and the unwillingness to deviate from the path before I reached the end. But on this trip, having embraced an openness to seek answers from within, I took the time to listen to my inner voice.

I obeyed unfamiliar internal nudges that led me down streets to places I had never been; there, I had encounters with people who taught me things about myself I had forgotten or never knew. And I experienced "coincidences" that defied explanation.

I was exposed to philosophies and ideas about love and peace and acceptance that I had never even considered before and that I'd never even thought I was missing in my life.

While some theories and teachings may take years to learn and absorb, I experienced instantaneous knowing and understanding, almost as if I was remembering something I'd forgotten. They resonated within me and created instant change.

I write this to show you that this can also happen to you.

By simply slowing down and looking inward, over the course of only four days, I had a complete shift in mindset. And in the end, I was left with two life-altering realizations.

The first happened at sunset at English Bay, as a light rain was starting to fall. I was sitting on a log, looking out across the water, when I was overcome with a sense of urgency to say something, but there was no one there to talk to. I took out my phone, pressed Record, and started speaking. I barely recognized the words coming out of my mouth. I pressed Play to listen to the recording and couldn't believe what I was hearing: a poem about love that I had composed.

How was a poem about love and peace coming out of *me*, the guy who others saw as removed and distant and sometimes not even very nice? The words and philosophies it contained were completely foreign and yet made so much sense.

I listened to it over and over, a question growing in my mind: If this had come out of me, then what else was in me that I didn't know about? This was really the start of my Who Am I? practice and the beginning of the answers that I would receive about my identity and my potential. At the time, I had no idea what was happening, but I was excited.

Aside from any mandatory poetry readings in high school, I had never in my life read poetry and certainly had never written any. How was it possible that this poem and the ideas within it had taken shape in my head and come out of my mouth so effortlessly? I asked myself how it was that I'd never known that I had these kinds of thoughts in my head. And why had I never known I had this ability to express them in this way?

The answer came to me: because I had never taken the time to know who I truly was.

It was like a giant lightbulb turning on in my head when I realized that I couldn't possibly feel engaged with my life when it wasn't even the authentic me living that life.

I had never allowed my truest self to be known to myself, to my family, my friends, or my teammates at work. The closest of them had seen some glimpses, but to most, I was the sports-loving, beer-drinking, chicken wing-eating, fast car-driving, self-centred entrepreneur who was hard to get to know or understand.

But how could they possibly understand me if I hadn't even taken the time to know and understand myself?

The next question almost knocked me down: If the people in my life didn't truly know who I was, then how could they ever truly love me?

Think about this in your own life for a minute.

We all want to be loved and understood. **But if you've never been the authentic, complete version of YOU, either with yourself or with those around you, then you have never really loved yourself or been authentically loved by those around you.**

The second realization happened on the plane journey home. Over just a few days in Vancouver, I had read about new ways of thinking and living that were already changing my life. I was starting to see a transformation in myself, through looking inward and taking the time to listen, and I wanted other people in my life to have the same experience. I couldn't wait to get home and share what I had learned and see others benefit from it.

What struck me was the strength of that emotion — that desire to see other people be engaged and excited about their work and their lives. What struck me was how much I deeply care for other people and what a profound desire I have to help others find their purpose, to see them succeed and be excited about their lives. It was mind-blowing to realize that I had never before expressed that level of care to people in my life, and I had certainly never been that sort of leader in my organization before.

Part of my disengagement at work had come from the disengagement I could see and feel in the rest of the team. What I really wanted was for each one of them to find their purpose and their passion and be actively connected and engaged with their jobs and the lives they were living. Everything I'd been reading and learning suddenly culminated in an understanding of what workplace culture is really all about.

To me, positive workplace culture is the secret sauce that so many leaders don't quite understand, but at the same time, is so highly attainable. The most intimidating aspect for most leaders seems to be just getting started. We tend to way overthink things and as a result, inevitably complicate it all.

"How can I possibly do what you have managed to do in your company, John? Where do we begin? How do we implement it? What does that look like?" These are the questions I hear all the time.

Recently, they follow up these questions with, "And how can I make changes in my personal life to heal and be so purposeful?"

What I discovered when I was in Vancouver answers all of these questions, and the most effective way I have found to explain it all is actually kind of simple:

It all starts with a seed of authentic care.

The seed of care is fundamental to the rest of the journey — a genuine care and love for yourself, for others in your life, and for people you can't even see but whose lives you touch just by your existence. The seed of care prompts you to want to make changes more than you want to stay with the comfort of the status quo (and, be honest, is that status quo even comfortable anymore?), and it steers you towards authenticity as a person. Caring for yourself and the people in your life, both at work and at home, and being willing to express that care, is all that's needed to start making changes that are profound.

To me, the seed of care meant that, as a leader, I wanted to show the people I worked with that I cared about them and wanted them to feel fulfilled and content in their work and in their personal lives.

To me, it meant that I didn't have to be distant or difficult to get to know and that showing care to people on my teams wasn't a sign of weakness but actually allowed them the freedom to also show care for each other and effect great change within our organization.

By expressing care for each other, we changed our bleak

outlook and stopped the in-fighting as a leadership team with one offsite meeting **in one day**.

We held a celebration for the entire company and unveiled our new workplace culture, changing the entire structure and manner in which we conducted our business **in one day**.

Our HR concerns dropped 85% in four months, and our growth, which had dipped below 10%, finished the year at just under 50%. Recruitment numbers soared as people heard about the changes and wanted to work for a company like ours. The press wrote articles about us that generated strategic alliances with companies who aligned with us because of the values we were now living out daily in our business behaviour.

These things are possible to achieve, and as leaders, we just need to believe that we, and everyone in our companies, can have it all. We can express genuine care and invest in the wellness of our employees and teammates and watch creativity and productivity soar. We don't have to rule with an iron fist or from a position of superiority as we have been taught for so long. These are false identities that we believe are important to wear as leaders (or as parents, as teachers, or from any position of perceived authority) but they are not. They may feed our egos and make us feel important in the short term, but ultimately, they weaken our relationships, destroy hope, and leave damage in our wake.

By failing to show care and empower your team, you are

telling the world that the only thing that matters is revenue and shareholder value.

But let me ask you this:

> Do you have low levels of engagement and are your people misaligned?
>
> Is it hard to recruit and retain talent?
>
> Is creative energy low or non-existent?
>
> Is it difficult to innovate in your company?
>
> Do people complain and are health concerns on the rise in your organization?

If you answered yes to any of those questions, and your organization is struggling, you will need to make many difficult decisions, and a lot of people will need to pull together and work hard to make changes. But for lasting change, I believe you must start by showing genuine care to each other and to your entire company.

Maybe you aren't a leader or in a position of authority, but as employees, too, we need to believe that we can have it all, that we can effect change both within us and around us by expressing care to ourselves, the people we work with, and the people we work for.

If you're showing up at work each day saying, as I did, "I don't want to be here," is it partly because of the lack of care you feel from your leadership? Could you start to make a difference in your workplace by showing care to your leaders and your teammates?

As individuals, we can all effect change in our families, our marriages, our friendships, and our lives by expressing genuine care for ourselves and others. We have such power, all of us, to impact the lives of the people around us on a day-to-day basis, both in our homes and in our workplaces, and I've seen firsthand the incredible change that can take place when you start to express care.

This book is not about theories or studies done at prestigious institutions.

It's about climbing back into our hearts and leading and living from them.

It's about listening, both to yourself and others, and engaging in meaningful practices that will start to change your life from the inside out.

It's about realizing that each company, each community, each family, and the people within them are all unique with one common thread: whether we are at home or at work, we just want to know that others care about us.

Whatever issues you may be experiencing personally or in

your family can be solved. Whatever issues your company or workplace may be experiencing can also be solved. Whatever issues individuals within your company may be experiencing can be solved, too. And whatever issues you are struggling with within yourself can be solved.

Grab hold of the sense of hope that comes with the knowledge that there are always solutions, even if the path isn't always clear or easy. Hope is so very powerful, and it will start moving you towards those solutions.

There are always solutions, and they begin with acting on the seed of care.

Acting on the Seed of Care

Having learned to see myself in a whole new light, I arrived home from Vancouver with a different mindset, resolved to make specific changes in my life. The version of myself that people had interacted with for so many years was going to fade away, and I was committed to discovering and returning to my true self and revealing that self to the world. I was going to start by showing care for the people in my life and by leading my company in a way that was authentic to me, in a way that made my team feel empowered and safe. I stepped back into my office, excited and engaged for the first time in a long time.

I picked up the phone and called my co-founder and CEO, a man I have been blessed to call my friend for over thirty years. We spoke for only a matter of minutes, as I told him what I wanted to do and asked for his backing and support.

"John," he said, "I don't know what this workplace culture thing is, but if you think it's important, go for it."

His belief in me brought me to my feet. "It's time to make changes and recapture our purpose and passion as a company," I said. "That's all I needed to hear. Leave it with me."

Words of encouragement are a form of care that is so very powerful.

To get started, I assembled the top-tier leaders and announced that we were no longer going to look at work as being separate from our personal lives. Sayings like, "It's not personal; it's just business" were to be wiped from our language. I shared my belief that our business needed to rediscover its roots and break down the misconceptions and misunderstandings between us and leave them behind us so that we could move forward together with success.

To show my leadership team that I cared for them as people beyond just their job titles and revenue-generating potential, one by one over the next few weeks, I met with key leaders who were having issues with the company and with each other. We had the difficult conversations we had been avoiding, about problems that were preventing us from being a unified team.

With those who wanted them to, these conversations went deeper, beyond just company issues and into our personal lives. We shared issues we were struggling with both at home and in the workplace. We listened to each other, expressed care and support, shed tears, and re-established trust, and I learned more about what was important to the people I worked with than I had over the previous five years. The change in the mood and the effectiveness of the communication among our leadership team was immediate and palpable.

No one is immune to the effects of being cared for. When we express care and support to those around us, it produces powerful and instant results.

It can feel overwhelming, wondering how you're going to act to show care to others. Instead, start by showing care to yourself by finding a place for daily retreat.

My retreat to Vancouver came just when I needed it, but afterwards, I still needed a space to go to for a few minutes every day, where I could reconnect to my dream of finding and expressing my authentic self.

Vancouver was an adventure for me, but you don't need to go across the world to find space in your life for yourself.

PRACTICE: Finding the Ten-Minute Spot

Background

When I was a kid, I didn't have a tree fort because my parents couldn't afford to buy me one. Instead, I would hide behind the raspberry bushes, eating all the raspberries, peeking out to watch my mother looking for me and imagining that I was in the biggest, coolest tree fort ever.

Sometimes I would play in the local corn field and dream about finding a tree in the middle of the field, with boards and a hammer and nails lying around it on the ground. I would imagine myself as a carpenter, able to build my own tree fort high in the tree.

Everyone needs a tree fort — a place where you can spend time alone, let your mind run free, and dream of all that could be. Everyone needs to find what I call the "ten-minute spot." The ten-minute spot is a place you can go to while you're driving home or out for a walk, a public place that you can get to quickly and that you can "own," even though it belongs to everyone.

My ten-minute spot is a few minutes from my home, near a river, past a field with massive willow trees. It's my clubhouse, my tree fort — the place I go to to be alone and do my "Who Am I?" practice.

Then I think about my day, my actions, how I reacted to situations, and whether they were in line with my WHO. I embrace love and self-acceptance, listen to the dreams of my heart, and imagine all that I can be tomorrow in a life filled with purpose and fulfilment.

That feeling you have in the morning when you get out of bed and know that today is just going to be about getting to tomorrow? That's the feeling of a life without joy and without purpose. That's a life in which every day is about doing what's expected and doing what needs to be done, with no real thought of what is being accomplished, who is being impacted, or how you're being improved. It's a life with unfulfilled dreams, devoid of adventure.

But when you care enough about yourself and are willing to invest the effort to actively engage with the adventure, you create a pathway from your heart for your dreams to travel down that actually enables them to become real.

When I was young, I used to spend time at a creek near my house. I could've stayed away from the creek, or stayed on one side of it, but instead, I consistently chose the adventure of jumping over the creek right at the point where there was a baseball diamond on the other side. I would sit and watch the older boys in my neighbourhood playing baseball, dreaming that I could be on their team when I was older.

One day, the coach called out to me, "John Stix! Come over here and take this mitt."

I was amazed. I didn't even know that he knew my name,

and now here he was calling me to join in and play shortstop for a game. I ran onto the field, grabbed the mitt, and took my position on the field, scared and excited. What a rush it was to catch that first grounder and throw it to first base. What an exciting, exhilarating, empowering moment — a dream come true. All from jumping a creek and dreaming. It's no surprise that my ten-minute spot is by a river.

Today's practice is to go on an adventure to find your ten-minute spot — a place you can go to and do your "Who Am I?" practice, a place where you give yourself permission to be completely yourself and where you feel free to dream.

If such a place is not immediately coming to mind, take a few moments to close your eyes and think back to your childhood.

> What did you dream of being when you were a kid?
>
> Did you dream of being a hockey player? Maybe your ten-minute spot is in the bleachers at the local arena.
>
> Did you dream of being
>
> > A rock star?
> > A doctor?
> > A politician?

In your childhood dreams, were you

Wayne Gretzky?
Wonder Woman?
Christopher Columbus?
Mother Theresa?

Where did you go to have those dreams?

Can you find a place like that today — a place where you feel free to dream, where you feel more creative, where you can retreat from the demands of the outside world and give yourself permission to be completely open?

Maybe you grew up in another country and can't easily get to your childhood spot or one like it. Can you set up a place in your home that reminds you of it or find somewhere local that you can imagine is that place back home?

Remember that the key to this early stage is openness to listen to your inner voice and discover your WHO. To do that, you need to take action and go on an adventure to find a place that's all your own and where you can be truly, fully you.

The Practice

Once you've found your ten-minute spot, spend a few minutes in the "Who Am I?" practice.

Then, express gratitude to yourself for caring enough to find this place and for showing up in it.

When you're ready, think about what it might look like for you to express care to others in your life.

I know that the thought of expressing care to others can be scary. Telling others that you care about them requires a level of vulnerability that you may not have with people in your life and you may feel awkward just coming right out and telling people you love them. Instead, think about actions you can take to show care and put a smile on someone's face.

There is not a single person in your life who doesn't want to know that someone truly cares about them. Start small and build confidence.

It can be
A sticky note on a colleague's desk at work
Flowers on your partner's pillow at home
Paying for coffee for the person behind you in line
Snacks for everyone at a team meeting

Do what's authentic to you and to the seed of care you've found inside.

STAGE II
Surrender is the Greatest Victory

"Surrender uncovers jewels along the path that you could not predict."

John Stix

CHAPTER 3: THE POWER OF VULNERABILITY

Vulnerability is a Strength

It's somewhat overwhelming, looking back, to realize the enormous changes that began with such a small surrender on my part. Sitting in my car, acknowledging, "I don't want to be here" was a huge moment of surrender, but a smaller, more profound moment had come the week before.

It was a beautiful summer evening and I was sitting on my deck with the BBQ going. The wind was blowing through the maple trees in the adjacent crescent, and behind me in the kitchen, my wife was chopping vegetables and I could hear the rhythmic slice and thud.

Frequently in those moments, I would contemplate the overall busyness of my day-to-day life and think,

Gosh, there's just got to be a way to have more of these moments of stillness and gratitude.

I'm not sure what was different about that night, but for the first time in my life, as I sat there listening to the chopping in the kitchen and watching the mesmeric movement of the maple leaves, I slipped into a meditative state.

Everything around me seemed to slow down as I said to myself, *John, there has to be more to all of this. Life can't be about anxiety and deadlines and racing between these small moments of peace and wholeness. There has to be more to life in a much deeper and profound way.*

A shiver came over me as an answer not only came into my mind but seemed to fill my whole existence.

There is more, John. I KNOW there's more.

That was a shift, a transition, and it's only now that I realize it was a shift as I look back and see all the changes that came after.

That was a moment when a phone was ringing in my life. I could've ignored it and that would've ended up just being a nice moment on my deck with the trees swaying in the wind, the sound of my wife in the kitchen, and the smell of the BBQ. Instead, I picked up the phone and answered it with a willingness to surrender to what that more could be.

Too often, we are taught that vulnerability is a sign of weakness and that surrendering means failure and defeat. We are taught that to recede means we've given up on the fight, given up on who we are. This is especially true for business leaders who are taught to always stand their ground and never back down.

I want you to know that what you've been taught about

vulnerability is false and that the purest form of surrender is indeed your greatest victory.

It takes strength to be vulnerable and it is through finding that strength and surrendering to vulnerability that your WHO can truly be freed.

Sitting on my deck, saying, "I KNOW there's more" was the first in a series of surrenders. It led me to sit in my car and be vulnerable enough to say, "I'm unhappy, disengaged, and passionless. I don't want to be here, and I can't continue to push forward in the same direction. It's not working. I have to give up and realize that I'll never feel engaged until I know who I am."

The "Who Am I?" practice is a practice of surrender that led me to a moment of awakening and self-awareness when I was in Vancouver.

When I called my business partner and said we needed to make changes in our workplace, he surrendered to my belief, allowing me to dive into an area of our business that I had not previously explored.

That step led to me being vulnerable enough to express my care to the leadership team, and to authentic dialogue and healing, and it started to break down the silos causing such dysfunction in our company.

When each member of the leadership team sat down and

surrendered to each other, measurable changes occurred in our business.

Rather than leading to failure, surrender and vulnerability led to incredible growth and victories. Ongoing surrender leads me to see the true dreams of my heart, and victory continues to confirm them. And it all began with that small moment of surrender on my deck, a moment where I heard a phone ringing in my life, and I picked it up.

Pick up the Phone

Imagine yourself walking down the path of your life. Along the path are phone booths, lined up, one after the other. And as you walk past them, the phone inside the first booth is ringing.

You have the choice to walk past or stop and pick up the phone. If you walk past, another phone booth with a ringing phone soon comes into view.

Sometimes the phones are harder to hear.
Sometimes you just ignore them.
But always, there's another one ringing.

These phones are connected to your authentic self, who has a message for you about your true purpose, who wants to tell you that the things you're chasing in life aren't connected to who you really are.

The more you keep moving along your path and ignoring

the phone, the harder it becomes to hear the ringing, until it's just a faint sound in the distance that occasionally breaks through.

Ignoring the phones is what leads to that initial sense of disconnection. It's what manifests the false relationships, the sense of unease and anxiety, the sense of feeling uncomfortable in your own skin, the behaviours that don't fit with who you are but in which you keep engaging, time after time, trying to feel something real.

The mind–body connection means these feelings and behaviours can manifest in chronic stress, tension headaches, or persistent pain. All of these disconnections are little rumblings along the path, like little earthquakes trying to move you closer to the phone, encouraging you to pick it up.

An exercise I often do with business leaders is to have them write down the names of five people who are important to them, and then write down five aspects of their lives that they really appreciate and wouldn't ever want to give up, aspects or activities that make them feel fulfilled and that life is worth living.

Then I ask them to give each person and each aspect on their list a rating from 1 to 10 or a percentage from 1 to 100 that reflects how much time they've spent with those people or engaged in those fulfilling activities over the past month.

It can be a sobering experience to learn that the people and the activities that they believe are important to them are often those they spend the least amount of their time with.

Try this activity for yourself during your time in your ten-minute spot, if you like. Look over the list of people and activities that you claim are important to you. Do you hear the phone ringing, telling you who and what you should be investing more of your time in?

Alternatively, think about something that you know is really important to you, something that resonates with you, something that when you see it or think about it or read about it in the news, can make you smile with joy or move you to tears.

Maybe you have a desire to eradicate violence and usher in world peace.

Maybe you have a heart for refugees
or people in poverty
or teenagers who are being bullied
or older people
or people who are ill and in hospital.

Maybe you're moved by animal rescue stories
or the sight of soldiers returning home to their families
or the look on a child's face when they learn something new.

Try to find what is at the base of that emotion.

Caring for others?
Reuniting families?
Fighting injustice?
Making sure everyone has enough?

Have you acted on this aspect of your life, even in a small way?

Have you acted on trying to bring about world peace just by offering love and peace to those around you?

Have you acted on your desire to help people who are sick, by volunteering in a hospital or taking a meal to someone who is housebound and struggling with illness?

If you take all your waking hours, what percentage of them is dedicated to animal welfare or helping people in poverty?

Why?

How do you know you care about this issue if you seldom do anything about it, when it's not the majority of your daily work?

> Is it something that gives you a heart-centred emotional response?
>
> Why does this issue connect so deeply — resonate at a deep, fulfilling, purposeful level — when you hardly expose yourself to it?

If it's so powerful that you know it's important even though you rarely do anything about it, that's your phone.

It's ringing.
It won't stop ringing.
Are you going to pick it up?

The phone is ringing to get you onto your path, and once you're there, you'll find something you absolutely love that you had no idea about. With it will come strengths and abilities you didn't know you had. You'll find healing that you didn't know you needed.

You'll meet people and become part of a bigger movement, learning and teaching and sharing. When you pick up the phone, you'll be connected to something that really deeply matters to you, matters to your journey, and puts you on a path to your WHO.

Walking along my own path, I couldn't hear the ringing of the phone, but I started to listen when I realized that the activities and achievements I had been pursuing were bringing me a false joy that was no longer enough. Even though I still loved all that we had built at work, I was feeling disengaged in my career and not bringing joy and passion to my personal life. I was empty and without gratitude. I didn't know that I was actually trapped in my own mind. I was thinking I couldn't be vulnerable — thinking, ***I can't let others know I'm feeling this way.*** Time and time again I told myself, ***It's just a phase and nothing is wrong. Just keep doing the things you don't like to do anymore, and eventually your passion will come back.***

Wow. That didn't make sense, did it? But isn't that so often what we do?

Even though we can feel the angst and negative emotions as they surface, we push it all down, refusing to answer the phones that are ringing and pleading with us to pick them up. We continue down that path of false fulfillment that is manifesting bigger and bigger issues in our lives and negatively impacting our mental health and emotional stability.

If we miss too many of these phones, do we get to the point where our foundation is shaken with a strong shake, with a life bomb? Quite possibly.

Life bombs can come out of nowhere and profoundly change us in a moment.

They disrupt.
They shape our future.
They blindside us.

Even if you can see them coming, you still can't predict their gravity, how they will hit you to your core and make you drop to your knees.

Life bombs are moments of brokenness and vulnerability that leave us hurting, lost, and disoriented. They make us want to go hide and isolate ourselves to deal with the emotions on our own. We don't share them, because we think that we're troubling others, or it's embarrassing, and we don't want others to know what we're going through. In reality, what we need most in those moments is a soothing, compassionate love — not to be told that everything is OK, but to be told that someone is holding our hand and we're not alone. That someone cares about us.

A life bomb can happen through no fault of your own and may be what caused you to develop a mask in the first place — a deeply traumatic event from your childhood that caused you to hide your true self away for fear of being hurt again. Or a life bomb can be life's way of telling you to pick up the phone when the little rumblings aren't working anymore; they can be life's last effort to show you how far you've come from who you are.

So why don't we pick up the phone?

> Maybe we're distracted by the busyness of the life we're living right now, mistaking busyness for satisfaction and achievement.
>
> Maybe we convince ourselves that this life we have is everything we wanted.
>
> Maybe we're afraid of the pain on the other end of the line — we're afraid of the surrender and vulnerability required to hear what our authentic self has to say. So we tell ourselves, "I don't feel entirely connected to this life I'm living, but it's OK. I'll just keep pushing forward and eventually I'll feel a sense of purpose and fulfillment. I'm fine."

Feeling "fine" appears to have become almost a goal in our society. It takes strength to be vulnerable enough to admit that, "I'm not fine. I'm not engaged and excited about this life I'm living. I am not the person who is living my life. The things I'm doing every day aren't adding value to my life or anyone else's." It can be hard getting to know yourself again, painful to work through the reasons why you're wearing your mask.

But I would argue that it's more painful to sit in a life that is devoid of purpose and dreams and adventure.

Take a moment now and imagine someone snapping a photo of you at the exact time when you decide to turn away from your ringing phone.

Looking at that photo, what does it say to you?

Are you happy?

Now imagine holding a photo album of your life. Do you want this photo in it?

So how do we pick up the phone and listen?

It starts with the "Who Am I?" practice. It starts with showing yourself that seed of care, by going daily to your ten-minute spot and taking time to listen to who you really are and to recognize the masks that have formed over your true self.

You'll begin to see the masks like mud, clinging to you, covering up who you really are. And as you peel off the mud, your true self will start to shine through. You'll have glimmers of dreams you used to have about the person you wanted to be and about the life you wanted to live that would bring you joy.

Part of showing yourself care is returning to your ten-minute spot, being vulnerable and open enough to remember those dreams, and then allowing your mind the freedom to imagine those dreams coming true.

Embrace the Power of Imagination

Imagination is a word we generally associate with childhood. We encourage children to use their imagination, but we never talk about how empowering it is for adults. In fact, even while we tell children imagination is fun, we also tell them it's not real, so we learn from an early age that we can't trust it.

We need to think past these labels we've put on imagination as being "not real" and "just for kids."

Imagination is actually an incredibly powerful tool that allows you visualize

all that you can be
all that you want to feel
and all that you want to achieve
and experience

Einstein called it a "preview of life's coming attractions."

Imagination will show you a vision of your possible future.

We become inspired by others who have big dreams and strong visions.

What's one of the most incredible speeches ever delivered? It's ***I Have a Dream***, by Martin Luther King, Jr. What does he talk about? He has a dream and he asks us to imagine the world that he can imagine.

When a leader describes a future that they believe can happen and that we're able to envision, it makes us believe.

It makes us say, "I'm voting for you, I'm following your ministry, I'm joining your company, I'm supporting your charity."

It's phenomenal to attach yourself to someone else's purpose and support them in it; that's the sign of a great friend, partner, or teammate.

But you also have the birthright and the ability to manifest your own destiny, by imagining all that you wish to infuse into the world, into the lives of the people you love, and into your own life.

Imagination is the birthplace of creativity and manifestation. It is your ability to imagine that frees your dreams and delivers them into reality.

When you were a child, that ability was so natural. Recently I was with a group of friends at my best friend's house. We were all in the basement, watching hockey and looking after all the kids running around.

One of my friends pulled out his cell phone and pretended to have a conversation. "What did you say? There's been a robbery? I'll send my best secret agent," he improvised, nodding towards his son.

His son instantly puffed out his chest, put his hands on his hips, and said, "I'm on it!"

What is it that my friend's son did? He immediately engaged with the idea of being a secret agent, immediately engaged with the dream. "Me? A secret agent? Why not? I'm in!"

As kids, it's so easy for us to jump into a dream world, embrace an identity, and run with it. It's so easy to surrender to imagination and dreaming. There's no effort involved.

When you were a child, you didn't have to think about who you wanted to be; you just knew what your dreams were, and it was an everyday part of life to act out them out and reveal your identity through daydreams and play. In imagining that you were a doctor, a restaurant owner, or an astronaut, you revealed your identity as a nurturer, an entrepreneur, an explorer. You revealed what characteristics you admired beyond just the person you were pretending to be, and you believed that you had those abilities and strengths to be what you could imagine.

This sort of effortlessness and playfulness is what you're aiming for as an adult — the ability to harness imagination again and hone it as a skill that you use to fully envision

a place you want to experience
a feeling you want to have
the way you want to live and communicate
the kind of relationships you want to have
with your partner, friends, and family
how you can love and be loved

With those imaginings will come little shivers of excitement, and thoughts of, *Could I really have this in my life?* Those shivers are the phone ringing, saying, *This is your dream. This could be your future. This could be yours.*

It was those shivers of purpose of wanting to see the people in my business be engaged and fulfilled again that led me to making changes in my work life but that ultimately led to deeper and more meaningful relationships with my friends and family and to new friendships. It's those shivers that led to me to making changes in my company that then led me to giving talks to other companies, to giving bigger talks, and to sitting here writing this book.

This moment, writing this book, is prosperity. It's a dream come true. How did it happen?

Because I imagined it. Imagination is the tool that enabled all these dreams to come to fruition.

Before a big talk, I'll go to my ten-minute spot and imagine that I'm standing on stage with an earpiece, looking out over an immense crowd. I feel a huge surge of love in the audience and there's an incredible energy of connectedness. I see it and feel it, and it's so real that it gives me shivers and makes me feel alive. It makes me believe that my dreams of seeing others find purpose and fulfillment can come true and that those dreams will bring a deep sense of my own purpose being fulfilled.

How often are we told that?

How often are we told that our dreams are actually connected to our purpose?

The feeling you get when you're doing something deeply meaningful, something that feels deeply purposeful and makes you feel more alive, comes because you've found a strong sense of who you are and you're acting out what you've found inside. In that moment, you've taken a leap of faith and jumped onto the path that is embedded in you.

You'll get shivers and goosebumps, and a sense of excitement and deep contentment, because the seeds of purpose in your heart are being revealed and starting to grow.

You won't experience that feeling with anything else except what's connected to your true self, whether that's

sharing a message on stage
baking bread
buying flowers for your partner
or bouncing a child on your knee.

Could it be that you can sharpen your ability to imagine all of life's possibilities and manifest your dreams based on what gives you those shivers?

We tell our kids that they can achieve anything they can imagine. As an adult, you need to embrace that idea and remember how powerful imagination is. You need to embrace it as

a tool for believing
a tool for having faith that something can come true
a tool for showing you a view of your dreams
and a possible future

The ability to imagine is a superpower that you should never give up, no matter how old you are.

Give yourself permission in your ten-minute spot to surrender to imagination, to practise remembering the dreams of your childhood and pay attention to the dreams that resonate with you today.

Practise remembering the dreams of your true self and listen for the phone ringing that says, "These dreams are yours and they can come true."

PRACTICE: Surrender to Dreaming

Background

Is there a phone ringing in your life?

Do you feel the rumblings?

Were you drawn to pick up this book or did someone give it to you?

Are you suffering from the stress and disconnection of daily living a duality, of not honouring your WHO?

Do you feel uncomfortable in the masks you're wearing?

Has a life bomb detonated, and do you not know how to deal with it or who you are as a result of it?

Is your business suffering, not knowing who it is or how to authentically communicate itself anymore?

It's worthwhile asking these questions about your business, because a business can wear masks and experience a false self, too. I saw it in my company, with everyone walking around, afraid to share, wearing their "work masks," and not wanting to express anything personal. It leads to disconnection, lack of authentic dialogue, and lack of passion and engagement. I've seen it within businesses that I mentor — businesses forget who they are and where they came from, and they put on masks to pretend that everything is all right and that they can keep pushing forward in the same way.

Through some sort of shaking, be it a quiet, ringing phone or a major life bomb, you have come to this place of recognizing that you are not living your authentic life, that there is a false mask covering your true self, preventing your real WHO from living outward. Through the "Who Am I?" practice, you're starting to get a glimpse of your WHO underneath the mask.

For me, that moment on the deck was a rumbling before the life bomb, a gentle shake that opened me up to possibility at a level I would never have imagined. Suddenly the unrealistic started to become possible. A seed of belief took root in me and it felt amazing.

It felt pure, bright, honest, and enlightening all at the same time. Within a moment of surrender and vulnerability, the path of living inward had begun in me.

Surrender is what allows you to acknowledge that you're wearing the masks and begin to look inward to take them off.

Surrender allows you to uncover parts of yourself you may not have seen in years, parts you may have forgotten about, and parts that are covered up by the masks, the mud, and the labels you've picked up and put on yourself.

I think a lot of us are carrying around negative labels that

our parents have given us
our friends have given us
our teachers and coaches have given us
and even that we have given ourselves

We choose to wear these labels that cover up who we truly are, and they hold us back from all that we can imagine becoming.

The only label that matters is the one you give yourself—the label that says you can achieve anything that you can imagine and that you know comes from your authentic self. Don't let others put labels on you that aren't consistent with who you are and that hold you back from all that you will become.

The Practice

In this chapter's "Who Am I?" practice, try to quickly work through the list of labels you can apply to yourself: I am a

partner
daughter
son
lawyer
cook
CEO

Strip away all the "things" that you are, by listing them off. Visualize each one as a little label that you pull off of yourself.

When you're done ask, yourself, "Who Am I?" again, going deeper this time, past the masks, past the labels, to the very core of you. Now, listen and watch for the dreams of your authentic self. Think about who you used to be in the ten-minute spot of your youth.

Who did you dream you could be?

> What superhero did you pretend to be?
>
> What rock star, or professional, or sports star did you dream you could be like?

Journal about the dreams of your youth. Be playful and creative with your writing. Write as if you are five or ten years old, writing about "what I want to be when I grow up." Write from that memory of being a young child filled with unrestricted dreams for the future, even seemingly impossible dreams.

Explore the heart of those dreams and what they're actually saying about who you were as a child and what you wanted to do and be in your life.

> Are they dreams of helping others?
>
> Dreams of creating and innovating?
>
> Dreams of travelling and exploring?
>
> Dreams of teaching and nurturing?

Which ones still resonate with you today? Imagine what having those dreams in your life would look like today.

When you were a child, imagination and dreaming were a form of self-care. Express that same care for yourself by being honest with yourself about who you are, what you dream about, what you want for your life and for the lives of those around you.

Practice remembering times in your life that were meaningful and purposeful to you.

> Who were you with?
> What were you doing?

In remembering those times, do you get little shivers of excitement, or a feeling of longing, or a sense of wanting to have that in your life again?

That's the phone ringing.

Surrender to the dream of what it would look like to have that sense of excitement and purpose in your life.

What would you need to have in your life to experience that?

Imagine what your life looks like with these dreams coming true.

> Who are you in your dreams of today?
> What are you doing?
> Who are you with?
> Who are you impacting and how are you being impacted?

When you imagine yourself — your deepest most purposeful self — imagine who that is, what you look like, who is supporting you in your effort, and who you can affect.

Imagine what your future could be — a future that is uniquely yours in which your seeds of purpose are able to grow and your dreams are able to be freed.

There is no judgement here or comparing yourself with what others have achieved. No one has set a standard or bar; there's no need to think you must achieve the same dreams that others have aspired to.

This is a time to attach yourself firmly to your own dreams and let your mind run wild with the possibilities of all there could be in your life, based on what gives you those shivers of purpose, those shivers that say, "this is for you."

CHAPTER 4: FEAR IS A LIAR

Let Fear Be the Passenger, Not the Driver

Up to this point, you might be thinking that I stepped off the plane from Vancouver and returned to the office with a detailed strategy, knowing exactly what I was going to say and exactly what I was going to do. It might sound like everything was incredibly easy for me and that at no point did I experience any doubts about where I was heading or any concerns about how to get there.

That couldn't be further from the truth. It wasn't easy. It required a willingness to let go of control and be vulnerable.

If surrender is your greatest victory and the doorway to your authentic life, then vulnerability is the key that unlocks the authentic version of who you are.

After my experience in Vancouver, I had no idea what was going to happen or how people were going to react to the changes in me. All I could do was embrace vulnerability and honour the commitment I had made to start revealing the authentic version of myself to those around me. I didn't know what would happen next or where this journey was going to lead and, right from the start, fear and doubt were my passengers.

That moment when I was sitting in my car, realizing I needed to stop looking outside myself to find answers, I felt incredibly alone and afraid. I thought I wasn't able or deserving enough to find happiness or engagement in my life again. Over and over, doubt slammed into me.

I had thoughts like:

> How do you think you're going to change yourself and show your true self to the world? Easier said than done, John.
>
> Who are you to think you'll be able to change to that degree? No one will understand what you're trying to do. You're going to lose everything you've built and lose all the people who are important to you.

During the changes we went through in our company, I was going through a profound transformation as a person. People in my life perceived me differently. I wondered what my family, friends, co-workers, and business associates were thinking, and I worried about how my relationships with them might change.

Even now, before every speech I give, and before I consult with a company, I still feel nervous. I wonder how people will receive what I'm going to say. Doubt gets in there and says, "Sure, you did it before, but do you really think you can do it again?"

Each time fear and doubt show up in my life, I gather up just enough confidence and courage to keep moving forward. Every time I do, my fears turn to focus. I remember my dreams, I remember that what I'm doing is directly connected to my identity and that my identity is connected to my purpose and my potential, and then I act. And with the action comes growth.

Fear is a great barometer for telling you that growth and breakthroughs are on the horizon. Fear never shows up when you're comfortable, when you're sitting on your couch, watching TV, not moving forward. It's when you get off the couch, hop in the car, and chase after a new challenge that fear hitches a ride in the passenger seat.

It sits beside you, attempting to strip away your self-confidence, saying, "You can't pull that off. You can't change. You can't go after that dream. You can't have that conversation with that person. Don't do it."

The night before I started having the deep-dive talks with my leadership team, I could hardly sleep. I knew I wanted to throw out the stigma that said that, as a man, I couldn't tell people that I love them, that I care about them and want what's best for them.

I wanted to show my company the seed of care I had discovered in myself. I wanted to realize my dream of seeing our leaders and employees be successful and engaged once again.

But what was everyone going to think?

What were they going to say?

And what would I do next?

I tried to plan out every detail for every eventuality, but it was impossible. All I could do was surrender to the dream and to the openness I had discovered in Vancouver and keep moving forward. I had no idea where this was all going to lead. I just had to go into those meetings and let myself be fueled by my dream. Nothing seemed more important than that and I wasn't going to let fear get in my way or have anyone tell me my dream wasn't possible or believable.

How many times have you felt inspired or had passing thoughts and dreams that sent exhilaration through your body?

You get those tingles down your arms and you think, ***Can I really do this? Could I really have this in my life?***

But right after you think those thoughts, the doubt also rises, delivering a message that you're not able to accomplish those dreams, that they're not for you. You feel that others are worthy to chase their dreams — they're smart, good-looking, talented. But who are you to think you can do the same?

Do you look at people who are successful, the heroes who have achieved great personal victories and think that they have dealt with any less doubt, fear, or rejection than you have? A quick internet search will tell you how many times J.K. Rowling's first Harry Potter book was rejected, or how many games Michael Jordan has lost, or how Elvis was told he would never get anywhere with his singing.

The difference is that those people didn't listen to the lie that said, "That dream isn't for you." They saw the dream deep in their hearts and they began with a mindset of, "I am enough, and I can do it." They absolutely dealt with fear and doubt and rejection and setbacks along the way, but they had the courage to pursue their dream because they knew the dream was for them.

Your dreams are there for a reason. They are your heart's innermost desires, making you the person most worthy to chase them because they belong to you. They weren't given to someone else. They're yours.

That's *why* you get the goosebumps. That's *why* you get the excitement coursing through your body — because the dreams are coming from your heart and they are connected to your purpose. Knowing that they are yours gives you the courage to pursue them.

It takes courage to act in the presence of your passenger named Fear; without fear there is no need for courage.

Courage comes when you realize that fear is a liar.

Fear is false evidence that appears real, and it is trying to hold you back from great opportunities, trying to keep you from your true purpose, potential, and fulfillment.

Instead of letting it tell you to put on the brakes, let it act as the navigator who tells you you're on the right path. Allow it to add to the excitement and heighten your strength because it confirms that you're going in the right direction. The road you are travelling is yours and it's meant for you, and courage equips you with the inner belief that over the next hill lies your purpose in dreams and potential fulfilled.

This is where your ten-minute spot becomes so critical. It's where you go to constantly reconnect with your dreams. You don't even have to find your dreams; they're already there in your heart. All you have to do is remember and reconnect with them, surrender to them, and let those shivers of purpose fuel you with the drive and belief to take another step forward.

As you return to the ten-minute spot and take time to really listen, you'll discover that you are full of dreams; they are a personal gift waiting to be opened and only you can open them. Your dreams are released when you care enough for yourself to listen to the voice deep in your heart. They are spoken in a language that only you can interpret, and they begin to come true through the power of vulnerability. You don't need to have a plan all drawn up with a list of action points and due dates. You take a step of faith, believing that the dreams are yours, and then you just start moving.

Did you have a bike when you were a kid? Do you remember the feeling of getting up on a Saturday morning and having no specific plans? You just went to your garage, got on your bike, and the day unfurled from there. Your bike led you to experiences, exploration, sights, sounds, friendships, and places you could never predict. It led to freedom. Every time you got on your bike, you had faith that it would take you somewhere. You didn't have a plan; you just started with your bike. But it always led somewhere.

Your dream is your bike. You just need to get on and start pedalling, and the dream will carry you to the next point. Every time you went into the garage as a kid and picked up your bike with no real plan beyond getting on and riding it, you were in your ten-minute spot. As an adult, your ten-minute spot allows you to be free to explore the dream and see where it takes you, not try and direct the dream in the way you think it should play out.

Maybe the dream you've seen in your ten-minute spot is, "I remember being a kid in the kitchen with my mom. We used to bake bread together and I remember how much I loved to bake. I remember the smiles on the faces of my family members and the pride I felt when I served our homemade bread at dinner. I miss doing that. I miss bringing joy into other people's lives with my baking. I want to get back to baking bread again."

It may sound trivial. Your mind will throw up all kinds of criticism and fear.

> That's a ridiculous dream.
>
> Why do you think you were even any good at baking bread?
>
> It was actually your mom's recipe; she was the baker, not you.
>
> And what do you think you're going to do next? Sell it somewhere?
>
> What does THAT look like?
>
> Where will you sell it? What will your price point be?
>
> What does the packaging look like?
>
> You don't know anything about running a business.

It's amazing how our minds do this to us. We start with one small thing that we believe will bring us joy, and then our minds erupt with all the reasons why we shouldn't pursue it. Our dream gets smothered by the false belief that we have to have everything figured out before we can even start. We become paralyzed by the fear that if we don't have it all planned out then we're going to go wrong somewhere.

Grab onto the truth that fear is lying to you and that the dream embedded in your heart is for you.

You don't need to have every detail worked out right now.

Instead, come back daily to the ten-minute spot, reconnect to the dream, and then take a small step forward. Bake a loaf of bread for dinner or to share with people at work.

Don't worry about what your dream looks like five or ten steps from now. Learn to take account of your abilities and realize that you are equipped with all that you need.

Keep reconnecting to the dream, and then move forward in courage, with the knowledge that if this dream is embedded in you, then you have the ability to bring it to reality.

Take an Account of Your Abilities

I like to redefine the word *accountability* in a playful way, as "an account of your abilities." When fear and doubt tell you that your dream is unreasonable, or can't possibly be something that you could accomplish, say out loud to yourself:

> I love this.
>
> I am good at this.
>
> If my heart is turned towards something, it's because I'm already fully equipped to achieve it.
>
> I'm perfectly able to accomplish my dreams.

And then take a personal account of your abilities.

Think about what you are strong at, and what you would like to be strong at. What strengths do you think you need to achieve the dreams of your heart? Is it possible you already have these strengths, or that when you step forward in confidence and courage to start achieving these dreams, you'll find the gifts are already there?

Sometimes you can't even see the gifts until you start down the path. For example, I didn't ever want to be a public speaker. I didn't think I could ever write well enough to write a speech, let alone a book. But as I took off my own mask and began to see who I am and to see the dreams of my own heart, those gifts and abilities began to grow as well.

Some gifts will grow with the dream, and some gifts you are born with that you didn't even know you had. Express gratitude to yourself for giving you the gifts you need to achieve your dreams, even if you don't yet believe you possess those gifts. Your life will answer the gratitude with people, opportunities, teachings, and strengths you didn't know you'd find, and you'll experience excitement and exhilaration and a curiosity about what other gifts you possess.

When you imagine your dreams coming true, the shivers you get mean that those dreams are connected to your WHO, to your true purpose, and along with your dreams come the abilities and opportunities to achieve them.

You were not given those seeds of purpose within, without the ability to make them grow.

Believe that this dream is yours, take an account of your

abilities, and then put on your cape and be your own hero.

Who was your hero when you were a kid?

How did it feel to be inspired by your heroes and the incredible things they did, to have the belief that one day you would also do incredible things?

Being the hero of your own journey is about surrendering to the dream you have discovered in your heart and being true to yourself and to that dream. It's about remembering who you've found yourself to be and consistently returning to the ten-minute spot to check in with yourself and reconnect with your dream. In doing so, you'll find the inspiration that will allow you to surrender and to have faith. Not faith in a plan of how you're going to accomplish your dream, but faith in yourself, in expressing what matters to you, and in your abilities.

It will be scary, because vulnerability is scary.

Our ego and pride and desire to plan and control everything gets in the way. Our fear of what others will think of us gets in the way. But again, it's that fear of what others will think and what society will think that tells you you're on the right track.

Have you ever heard of social scripts? I find these very interesting. Imagine you've just entered an elevator full of people. You're probably not going to sit down. Everyone stays standing because we've all agreed to a certain set of social behaviours for that environment. We have social scripts that tell us how to behave in a predictable way and one that doesn't make others uncomfortable.

We feel more comfortable when we know how we're supposed to behave; we get nervous going into situations where we don't know what is expected of us. When we behave in a way that goes against our society's scripts, we often experience embarrassment. The fear of embarrassment or judgement keeps us from doing even socially acceptable things, like dancing at a party or singing karaoke. It can keep us from doing things that could actually bring us joy and fulfillment.

Ask yourself: Is there something you know is connected to your happiness that you would do only if you knew you would never be judged for it?

Put another way, I once heard someone ask, "If you were asked to be ten times bolder, who would you be and where would you be in your life?"

Jot down what came to mind for those two questions. If you have anything to write down, then you have room in your life for growth and greatness.

> When you think about going after your dream, are you worried that others will judge you for it?

> Are you being held back because you're afraid of failure?
>
> Is it possible you're holding yourself back from doing something that is actually aligned with your WHO?
>
> Is it something that could bring joy to you and to others?
>
> Is it possible that you, like a hero, are meant for greatness?

Living inward is about acknowledging the greatness within. It's about shedding the ego to remember your true identity instead of choosing or creating an alternate version of yourself. As you shed your false self, you'll see seeds of purpose, seeds of your truest potential. And as you remember who you are, you'll find the ability and the greatness to nourish those seeds and bring them to fruition.

Sometimes I watch motivational speakers or celebrities who talk about their successes, and the advice they so often give is, "Just decide to do it and then go for it." How many times have you heard someone tell you to "just go for it" and it didn't feel right to you, or you felt "less than" because of that statement? You felt encouraged but only for a short time, because then you felt lost about what "it" was that you were supposed to go for.

When you go through this process of living inward to find

out who you truly are and what truly matters to you, you'll just be living *you* and you can "go for it" with confidence, knowing what you're going for and why.

It will be completely natural because you'll take what you've found in your heart and start living it outwards and you'll be so engaged with what you're doing, and so in love with what you're doing, that there will be no decision to be made and no need to frame your mind to go after it. You won't need to get up day after day making that decision and motivating yourself to "go for it" because you'll just be living YOU and it will be the most natural and fulfilling thing to do.

Remember to stay connected to the seed of care that you've found for yourself and others, to keep ego and agenda at bay. Stay connected to the fire burning deep inside.

Remember that surrender is victory, and you are victorious when you are surrendering to who you are, your dreams, and what matters in your heart. The vulnerability comes in revealing who you are to others — in telling your partner or your friends that you want to bake bread and then just getting started doing it.

You might be surprised at the reactions that you get. When I went to my business partner and said, "Our business is suffering and it's my dream to express care and love," that was me saying, "I want to bake bread."

When I said, "I don't know exactly what that's going to look like, but I just need to do it," that was me saying, "I don't know what I'm going to do with all the bread I'm going to bake, I just need to start baking."

When you begin to reveal your authentic self, incredible changes take place. Those around you will support you, and you'll be free to be more creative and motivated to make more changes. In my case, the support my friend gave me was liberating and empowering.

Your partner or friends may similarly surprise you by saying, "Oh yeah, I remember that bread your mom used to bake and I've been hoping you would bake that same bread for me one day."

Or they may say nothing at all. Some of them may look at you like you're crazy. "What are you talking about? You've worked for this company for twenty years making a good salary and now you want to give it up to bake bread?!"

I definitely got some puzzled looks when I first started expressing love and care to people at work. I'm sure some of them were thinking, ***What is he talking about? We have a business to run and serious problems to figure out and he wants to sit and chat about what's going on in my life?!*** Not everyone necessarily believed me or knew what to do with what I was saying, but no way was anything going to stop me from telling people that I cared about them.

This is where the ten-minute spot is critical. When you

know that what you've found in your heart is real and authentic to you, continually returning to the ten-minute spot reminds you of the dream and gives you the belief and inspiration to keep doing it. In the process of expressing your dream, roadblocks and setbacks will cause you to forget the inspiration. It's not always going to come easy. It's going to take a lot of work.

The ten-minute spot reminds you that nothing is going to stop you because your dream makes you feel so alive and because it's connected to your purpose. Your ten-minute spot is your reinforcement. It's your gasoline. It's the place you come back to and where you shake off procrastination, fear, and judgement of yourself and from others. It's where you embrace belief in the dream no matter what reactions you receive or what roadblocks get in your way.

Your ten-minute spot is where you tell yourself you are able, because you know this dream was made for you. Like your fingerprint, your dream is unique to you, which means you can't necessarily expect others to feel it or understand it.

The strength that holds you to your own purpose is not your own strength, or even other people's strength, but the strength of WHO you really are.

Your ten-minute spot is where you go to continually reconnect to that purpose and then act. And then reconnect and then act. That reconnection will help you run and soar, and then people around you will see what you're truly doing.

They'll hear the passion in your voice. They'll see how all of this is leading you to be more of the authentic you. And then you'll find family and friends supporting you in a way you didn't expect.

After our company's massive cultural shift, my CEO came to me and said, "Why aren't you president?" He may not have understood what I was setting out to do at the beginning, but it didn't take long for him to see the passion and the results, and for him to suggest that I take on a new leadership role, although that was not a result I had even considered at the start of my journey, nor was it even a part of my dream. My dream was to show others that I care, to lead in a way that was authentic to me, and to share a message I thought everyone needed to hear about the importance of discovering your true identity. The incredible changes in our company were the outcome of my dream and the dreams sparked in the leaders around me.

When you start off baking bread, you're not thinking about winning the Best Bread in the County award; that kind of result takes care of itself and even becomes somewhat irrelevant when you're feeling fulfilled. When you love yourself enough to chase your dream, the reason you love what you do is because of your love for yourself and your love of pursuing the dream.

PRACTICE: Express What Matters to Those That Matter

Background

To start manifesting your dream, ask yourself, What is the seed of care you've found through the "Who Am I?" practice? What is the dream that's being refueled each time you return to your ten-minute spot and allow your imagination free rein? Now, how are you going to act on the seed of care you've found for yourself and others? What is a small step you can take towards surrendering to the dream? A good place to start is by expressing what matters, to those who matter in your life.

This is a practice to embrace when you've had several sessions in your ten-minute spot of the "Who Am I?" practice, remembering and journalling about dreams of childhood and youth, and imagining dreams for your life now.

Within the prison of the shadow self, you created elements of your life that are false. As you are uncovering your authentic self and remembering dreams that matter, your shadow self will generate fear. It will try to hold you back by telling you, "You can't accomplish that. Who are you to think that you can amount to anything great? You can't achieve this dream that inspires you because it's just a dream and therefore not attainable."

Will you choose to grab your seeds of purpose and choose

to believe that you are born for greatness? Thank the fear for showing up and confirming that you're on the right path. Grab onto your dream and know that it's even more than a dream — it's your destiny.

Think about it this way:

> Wouldn't you want this for someone you love?
>
> Wouldn't you want them to be the best and most authentic version of themselves, guided by their personal values and purpose to reach their fullest potential?
>
> Would their greatness take away anything from you?
>
> Or instead, would it be greatness for everyone around them who authentically cares, including you?

Those who authentically care about you want your dreams for you, and they want to support you in those dreams.

The purest potential of the authentic you is ready whenever you are. Start with a willingness and let your faith in who you really are come alive; let it unleash and soar. It doesn't matter if your purpose is to be the best mother, the best gardener, the best baker, or the very best at anything, as long as it's connected to your true self. As long as you are no longer listening to the doubt and the doubters. As long as you break free from the strongholds and the fear holding you back from all your purpose, all your happiness, all your joy, all the peace that already belongs to you. It's yours and it always has been.

Put yourself out on your own personal stage and love yourself every day for doing it. I know I will be loving you from afar for being brave and courageous and for fighting the good fight.

You deserve you!

The Practice

Spend your quiet time today thinking about the dreams you've remembered and uncovered, dreams connected to your purpose and your authentic self.

What would you say to someone really close to you about what you have found that matters to you so much as an individual? Your journal is a safe place to start formulating this conversation. Write out the conversation you want to have with this person about what you've found. Journal about the key elements of the conversation.

In visualizing this exchange, fear may enter, but remember that you are safe because you are authentically expressing who you are, and because you know that fear is the passenger whose presence you can use to encourage you, not stop you. So let it be the passenger.

You don't need to actually have the conversation right now.

Commit to remaining open and listening to that voice inside you — it's revealing who you are and what's truly important to you. As you start to hear what matters to you as an individual, and you embrace the vulnerability to go further into yourself, you'll know when it's time to start expressing yourself to the people around you.

You deserve to feel authentic. You deserve to feel that you can be who you are, especially with those whom you love. You deserve to feel relaxed and peaceful within who you are, and you achieve this by first discovering your authentic self and then having the courage to express who you are to the people who matter in your life.

I'm not saying go tell the world. You don't have to tell sixty people about what you've found. This is a soul expression of the things that really matter to you and you need to be vulnerable with a few people you respect and who are going to accept you. This is the beginning of aligning the inner you with the outer you — the start of small life changes that will reap huge rewards.

When you're ready, tell someone you trust, so that you can experience success the first time. Express yourself to someone who will fully accept where you are and not be afraid of what you have to say or try to turn you away from the path you're on. Take a small step and express yourself to those who are important in your life — those who will receive what you have to say and provide you with a sense of safety.

To get started, pick something you've heard from that voice inside that really resonates with you, something you know is connected to your dream. A lot of people feel disconnected in their careers, and the idea of "baking bread" (or something like it) may really speak to you. But maybe your dream is connected to the kind of relationship you want with your partner or with an old friend.

It doesn't have to be something big. It could be something as simple as, "Why did I stop playing tennis? I love it. I played it as a child and again through university. I had a lot of friends who played tennis and it was a key part of my social life and I lost touch with some good friends because I stopped playing. Why did I do that?"

The vulnerability comes with being able to express that to people who matter and will hear that. You need to be able to say to your partner, "Look, honey, I've been thinking… remember my friend Doug? I never see him anymore. I miss that interaction. I feel like I want to get back to that. We used to play tennis together and then the kids came along, and our lives got so busy that I let it drop and I really miss it. And with our current finances, I'm not sure we can afford to join the club where I played before, but I want to tell you how important this is to me."

This path won't lead you to play tennis as a pro — it's a step along your path. In remembering how much you miss your friend and that activity, now you need to be vulnerable enough to express yourself in a loving, kind way, and be heart-centred in how you tell people. Express yourself in a way that shows you are vulnerable and encouraging authentic dialogue.

"I love tennis and I would love to get back to playing it. Is there room in our life for that?"

Or, "I love baking bread and I want to get back to that. Is there room in our meal planning for me to bake bread a few times each week?"

Be vulnerable about the things that matter to you and express those things with a seed of care, while honouring your authentic self.

CHAPTER 5: LOOK BACK AND HEAL

Looking Back

During the deep-dive talks among the leadership team, it became increasingly clear that we didn't understand our corporate identity or our corporate purpose. The leadership silos had already started to crumble and the dysfunctional working relationships were beginning to fall away. But we agreed that the only way to continue moving forward was to take off the corporate mask and show our customers who we were.

Because a corporation can wear masks just like people can. We had taken off our masks with each other; now we needed to remove the corporate mask to remember the WHO of the business, so that we could align our business behaviour with the business WHO and make real changes.

I personally was starting to see the changes that were taking hold in myself and in my life by asking myself every day, "Who am I?", and I theorized that finding our company's WHO would allow us to address and break down both the internal and external barriers to growth.

I booked an offsite location where we could meet and

engaged an external consultant to help us through the process, knowing that I couldn't be the one to lead us; we all had to sit together as equals and be able to present equally respected opinions.

I'll never forget that day. Even before it started, I felt such a sense of belonging and purpose, with all of us joining together to decide the company's future. Until that day, our company had always operated with a very top-down approach. We weren't used to having collaborative discussions when making critical decisions, and I anticipated many disagreements, but I also had a hope that in coming together for this critical step, we would be able to move forward together in the right direction.

As anticipated, the day began with awkward, quiet moments filled with tension, and a frequent need for breaks, but slowly throughout that single day, the vulnerability and deep seeds of care in all of us inspired amazing contributions. As people felt heard and safe enough to share, unification occurred, ideas started to flow, and we scrambled to write them down fast enough. The hours disappeared as we covered the walls in sheets of paper filled with deep creative expressions of who the company was.

By the end of the day, we had established a whole new set of core values and our company purpose. I remember us all with huge smiles as we paused to reflect on how incredible the day had been and to rejoice in the sensation of old friendships being renewed. In being vulnerable to each other, we had increased trust and safety and set our company on a whole new path.

An important step in coming back together had been to reflect on how we had managed to become fragmented in the first place. Throughout the deep-dive talks and the offsite, the story emerged of how we had managed to shift from a tight-knit group in a basement to an organism of a couple of hundred members. In telling the story of our history, we saw how we had moved up the leadership ladder and lost connection along the way with who we really were and with those around us.

By sharing the challenges we had faced, and the wounds we had sustained, we acknowledged the masks we had put on to cover our scars. We identified what had contributed to the misunderstandings and the hooks that had pulled us towards dysfunction. We learned about being vulnerable enough to share our journey with each other, offer forgiveness, and experience healing.

We learned the power of storytelling.

Embrace Storytelling

Storytelling is an ancient practice that reminds civilizations of where they came from, who they are, and what they have suffered through and triumphed over, and it explains the values and rules they guide themselves by today. Stories provide a sense of identity, connection, and belonging. To truly understand a society's present, you need to hear about its past.

The same is true for companies and individuals.

When I moderate other companies' offsite realignment retreats, one of the exercises is to Embrace Storytelling. I ask each of the leaders present to tell the story of how the company came into being and how they came to be connected with it. The leaders talk about their roles and how they've changed, what changes they've seen take place within the company, and who they feel the company is now. It allows everyone to come to agreement about the history of the company, who the company originally was, what its original purpose was, what challenges it has faced along the way, what scars it has accumulated, what masks it has put on to protect itself and, consequently, where it has ended up today.

Storytelling reveals why the leaders behave as they do, what is holding them back, and what they need to forgive and release in order to move forward. Through storytelling, they are able to honour what is true, take it forward and evolve, and leave behind what is unnecessary.

At the time, we found storytelling to be so integral to establishing a connection between new employees and our company that we implemented a "Culture University." When new employees joined our company, we shared the story of the company's history, explained what it means to be "IN", defined our purpose and values, and handed out declaration cards and "I'M IN" T-shirts. Hearing about the organization's past helped new employees to understand who the organization is now, what direction it's moving in, and why we make the decisions and engage in the behaviours that we do.

Storytelling is equally important for us as individuals.

During our company's offsite and the examination of our company's past, I realized the need to examine my own past. I had been daily asking, "Who Am I?", and I was confirming more of what I had learned about myself in Vancouver. I found something in my heart that I didn't know was there, and as I expressed more of my authentic self to people around me in my life and at work, I saw a ripple effect as others felt empowered to do the same. It was sparking creativity, authentic care, and compassion and making a difference in my family life and in my relationships with friends and work colleagues.

All of this raised the question: What had stopped me from doing this before?

This true version of myself was being so well received and causing such incredible change and transformation that I had to wonder why I hadn't been like this all along. How did I not just instinctively know who I was before? Why was this other version of myself even out there to begin with?

In the midst of all this euphoria about what was happening at work, I felt guilt and regret that I had lived so long without knowing and expressing my own identity. I became curious about what had shaped me and brought me to this point. That's when I embraced storytelling and started to look back.

It's not really surprising that I ended up being a co-founder of a communications company. Growing up, I was the youngest of four boys. There was a large gap between myself and my three older brothers, so they understandably were always off on their own adventures and had a hard time relating to me. My dad, Edward, was a sales manager, who left early in the morning, came home for dinner, and then went back to work until after I was asleep. My mom, Kay, was loving and nurturing, but she was busy raising four boys and holding down a part-time job for extra income. My early years were spent just trying to be seen and heard by people in my family who either weren't there or were just too busy.

When I was seven, my parents divorced, and I moved with my dad and one of my brothers into a basement apartment in Waterloo. My mother stayed in town for a while and then moved to Toronto with my twin brothers. Her emotional and physical presence in my life faded, and for the next eight years, I saw her mostly only on Christmas Eve.

My dad was amazing — he was my rock — but where he had been busy before, now he had even less free time, trying to hold down his job and figuring out how to raise two boys on his own. He started a nightclub in Toronto, which was a success, but in the early years it meant he was away most

Friday evenings. He would ask my older brothers to come over and babysit, but all three of them were teenagers with their own plans, and often they didn't show up or would leave early. I ended up spending many nights alone, huddled on the kitchen floor, scared of the dark and the strange noises that came from the factory behind us.

At school, I had trouble focusing. I had no close friends and, while I wanted to be liked by everyone, I didn't know how to relate to my classmates, and my demands for their attention would often backfire. I dove into sports because it was something that came naturally to me, but I was a terrible teammate. I couldn't understand why everyone couldn't play at the level I wanted them to, so I was hard on everyone around me. I felt alone and misunderstood; I believed people would like me if they could just see the person I was inside, but I was always trying to get attention in the wrong ways.

My dad remarried and I frequently lied to my stepmother, telling her that my mom was coming to visit me. Maybe sometimes she actually was, but I think most of the time I was just looking for attention and sympathy.

I believe it was around that period when the masks really started to form, and as I grew up, the masks took hold. I felt I had to wear expensive clothes, drive fast cars, regularly go to clubs and parties, and do whatever it took to be noticed, to not be alone, to make people think I was a talented, successful guy, who had it all together.

But what I projected as my reality was actually a mask covering up the fear and pain and hiding the real me away from myself and from everyone around me.

Release All Hope of a Better Past

Embracing the stories of your own childhood is essential for seeing how those early years shape the masks and adaptations you think you need to exist in a normal way.

It's not a conscious decision to form these masks; I believe it's more of a coping mechanism. It's a natural extension of living an outward-focused life, in which we've grown up conditioned to believe that life is a series of quick movements from one place to another.

In the same way that companies can grow quickly, causing the leaders to lose sight of the business and each other, as we grow, so too do we lose touch with who we are. We put on masks to cover the hurt and pain of our experiences. We put on masks based on what we think we need, or what we feel is expected of us, and we begin to live as someone we are not. We all do it, and most of us don't even know we're doing it. These masks just form over us to cover up the pain. But they also cover up our true self, preventing us from loving ourselves and from being able to be truly loved by others, as we end up seeking love and acceptance in the wrong way.

It requires surrender to tell yourself the stories of your past and to recognize where the masks have come from. Surrendering will bring awareness to aspects of your life that aren't an accurate depiction of your true self, and often, it feels bad to find out that you have tendencies and habits that are not representative of you and are holding you back. It's painful to confront memories from your past that have manifested your masks.

But these aspects are holding you back from so much enjoyment, so much possibility and abundance in your life. They hold you back from having genuine relationships with others and from living the life that's filled with what matters to you as a person.

When you find the courage to release them, you're freed to live a joyful, abundant life. Surrender allows you to acknowledge them and release them from a place of love for yourself, for all that you are and can possibly be.

You don't have to be critical or hard on yourself. So many of us have an expectation that we should be perfect, but it's your imperfections that highlight your own beauty. Without the opposite, there is no comparison. You just need to realize that the imperfections and masks in your life occurred for a multitude of different reasons, but it is within your power to now say, "I let go these aspects of who I am with self-love, so that the real version of me can surface and shine more for others."

To let these aspects go, don't fight with yourself or put yourself down because you have them. In fact, realize that they helped create you in this moment. But you don't need them anymore — you have an awareness of them, so you let them go without judgement or guilt. You let them go from a place of love because you have compassion for your past self and you can forgive yourself and others.

I personally went through a stage of being mad at myself, pointing at things in my past and saying, "That's a terrible thing to have done or said or thought."

And then my dear friend, whom I call Mrs. T, said to me, "Wait a second, John, why are you doing that? You love yourself enough to notice that they're there. Now love yourself enough to just let them go."

Too often, we drag our past into our present moment and impose judgement on ourselves for our past imperfections. But this self-punishment is a form of a lie. It's not what anyone who loves us would want for us. It's not what our true self wants for us.

And yet the punishments live on, and we experience guilt by holding onto past situations. We bring them into the present moment, making them real again and blaming ourselves for decisions made long ago. We experience regret by holding onto what could have been and believing the lie that our best is behind us and our opportunity for greatness has passed.

We experience shame — that horrible feeling of error in our lives and the belief that what we've done is worse than what anyone else has ever done. It makes us afraid to take risks, in case history repeats itself. It tells us that others think the worst of us and will never give us a second chance.

We experience loneliness and feel that nobody understands us — that we're separated from everyone and that we must be the only person who lives and feels this way. We think no one else could possibly identify with us or even care to do so. We look around and see everyone else with someone to confide in who understands them.

We become paralyzed by worry. Our minds ruminate on all that could possibly happen, and we're unable to make decisions or commitments because of all the things that could go wrong. Thoughts run through our minds faster than any possible outcome could be developing.

All of these emotions send our minds swirling into the past, dragging our history into the present and shaping our future by making us panic into action or inaction from a place of fear. It keeps us from a state of peace, and we become anxious and depressed.

You're not alone in experiencing these emotions; we all have them. I battle guilt and fear and anxiety. I battle thoughts that tell me I need to be more or I'm not good enough to deserve happiness or contentment.

In my early forties, after my mother died, I thought a lot about how I hadn't done enough for her, how I should've got up earlier to spend more time with her in the mornings, how I didn't cook with her often enough, how I could've done more in that time when we all still lived together.

All of this is a trick and deception of the false self. They're distractions and tools of the false ego that say, "You're not going anywhere. You're going to stay here in this prison of negative thoughts and memories. I'm going to manifest them, and your mind is going to ruminate and enter into depression and anxiety so that you stay trapped in the past and can never move forward."

It's a lie that you have to hold onto the pain of the past. It's a distraction that keeps your eyes off of your true self and keeps you from realizing your dreams and your true potential. In the present moment, you feel pulled back in time to relive the hurt all over again.

Why?

> Because you deserve to?
> Because it feels good to be angry and in pain?
> Because you don't deserve happiness?

The true cause of these emotions is that you haven't forgiven yourself for past aspects of your journey, where you feel like you've failed or that someone has failed you.

It's so freeing when you understand that the guilt and shame and anger you feel are simply manifesting from a time that no longer exists. The emotions you feel don't own you — they aren't your identity. They existed at one time, but they belong to a moment in the past. In dragging the past into your present, is that moment happening all over again?

No. It's not.

The lie is that you need to continue to feel a certain way about something that happened in the past. The lie is that those emotions belong in this present moment.

And once you are aware of those lies, can you love yourself enough to embrace the truth that you deserve to let them all go?

When you give up all hope of a better past, you can release the blame and punishment of the false self and embrace who you are now, finding freedom in self-forgiveness. It is your greatest gift to yourself, timed exactly when you need it. It's selfless to offer and yet so self-nourishing. As you make efforts to truly forgive, you show yourself that you love who you are at your core enough to say goodbye to the pain.

Forgiveness is the key to open up your heart and experience freedom and healing.

Healings and Micro-Healings

I have no memories of the day my family was split apart. I don't have any recollection of the move or of the days leading up to it. It's just completely blank. Where did that memory and that original pain go? Will I ever be able to remember?

Many years later, I've come to the point in my life where I'm attempting to look at those memories of being separated from my mother, of being alone so much of the time, of nights when my dad was working and my brothers didn't show up — nights spent on a cold vinyl kitchen floor, too afraid to move. I continue to unpack those memories and in doing so, I continue to experience healing. I know there is more healing to come, and I remain open to it. This is a daily mantra for me, and I've learned that healing can show up at any time.

One evening, my wife and I were watching *A Monster Calls*, a movie about a boy dealing with his mom's terminal illness. The boy, bullied at school and part of a fragmented family, is alone a lot in his life. One day, with no one else to turn to, he starts talking to a tree, which talks back, telling him stories that change his life.

In watching the movie, I related to the boy and his loneliness and fear of losing his mother, to the point where I had tears in my eyes. *What is going on?*

My wife, in her gentle wisdom, told me what I needed to

hear. "I'm not sure why, but I feel like you need to go to your mom's gravesite."

I drove out to the cemetery and sat by my mother's grave, thinking of my parents. As a child, I'd never thought of their breakup as a tragedy or believed that their divorce bothered me or affected me very much. As an adult, that memory was so far in the rearview mirror of my life that I had no reason to think about it or see it as a possible problem, so I'd never talked about it. I never realized how that part of my childhood had contributed to the masks I used to cover my authentic self. It took a movie about a young boy dealing with his mother's death to take me to my own mother's gravesite. I knelt down and mourned my parents' divorce, mourned how it had impacted me. By her side, I found healing and I was able to forgive.

What was it that erased the hurt and brought healing?

> The realization that the pain of my childhood had shaped me.
>
> The realization that I did nothing wrong.
>
> The realization that giving up all hope of a better past is the first step to forgiveness.
>
> The realization that I am not on that cold floor any longer and that I will not let that fear grip me for one instant longer.

> The realization that I love myself enough to forgive it all, including fear itself.

I will not let it shape me or keep me from my true self and my future. Instead, I will be thankful for it, because it brought me to this point of being able to love myself, shaped for who I am in this present moment. In delving into my past, I was able to understand the masks I was wearing, why I was wearing them, and why I needed to be noticed.

The healing process helped me to better define who I truly am, but it doesn't happen all at once. Part of the journey is recognizing that there are stages you'll move through, but it's not cut and dried. Completing a chapter or a practice in this book and moving through a stage doesn't mean you'll never revisit it, and experiencing healing doesn't mean there isn't more healing to come.

All of the practices in this book are meant to be experienced over and over. There's a reason it's called *living* inward. Living the inward journey every day means remaining in a state of openness and a state of surrender to experience ongoing micro-levels of healing for events in your past, sometimes ones you thought you had moved past, forgotten, or didn't even believe had impacted you. Micro-healings will happen in current relationships with friends, family members, and colleagues, at home and at work, at times when you least expect them.

As you progress, you're being freed from the constraints of the false ego; you're shedding masks that will reveal another layer to heal from. Repeatedly on this journey, you will have to let go, give up control. It's unsettling, but this surrender is what allows you to progress inward without judgement, knowing it's OK to not be perfect, and accept that your mistakes can be as beautiful as your joyful successes.

As you go deeper in the "Who Am I?" practice, you will get flashes of things that hurt, pain from the stories of your past and your present. You will be tempted to turn away. But go deeper and you will continue to find little glimpses of your true self and you will understand why the false ego generated false versions of yourself to sit in front of the real you.

By being vulnerable you'll see the lies that are there, logjamming the real you. You will experience moments of healing that are unique to you and what you've been through. These moments are beautiful, and they happen with a gentleness that no human counsellor or friend could ever bring. They rise up from deep inside your heart and manifest out to contribute to the process of healing as they move you gently closer to forgiveness and self-acceptance.

PRACTICE: Embrace Storytelling and Surrender to Healing

Background

As you spend time in your ten-minute spot, feeling joy and exhilaration as you connect back to the dreams of your youth, you may wonder what held you back from pursuing those dreams before.

What was it that trapped you?

As you release what's in your heart and see the changes in your life and the lives of those around, you may start to wonder why you never did this before.

"What shaped me? The life I'm living is not in line with the dreams I used to have and the person I dreamed of being. How did I get here?"

It's important to explore those questions because as you're chasing your dreams there will be hooks and setbacks trying to revert you to your false self. By embracing storytelling, looking back, and healing, you'll understand what caused you to adopt the masks, and through forgiveness of yourself and others, you will release the power the hooks have to pull you back and trap you once again.

In embracing storytelling and looking back, retain an openness and a curiosity, rather than a mindset of blame or guilt. When we went through the offsite at our office, we realized we had masks that needed to come off. We had to dive into the stories of our past to discover what had led us to that point. We experienced healings and micro-healings in our workplace. We had leaders who said they couldn't get along, and then all of a sudden they were able to take off the masks and look at what had happened from a place of curiosity, of asking themselves honestly, "How did we get here?", without looking to blame anyone.

It disintegrated those old identities that we'd felt mattered and it freed us to look at how we'd behaved and why we hadn't got along. We realized we didn't have to act that way to protect ourselves or our silos anymore. As we supported each other and expressed ourselves with care, we felt safe to start unleashing what was in our hearts and it provided healing to our relationships. The healing and sense of safety allowed us to be vulnerable enough to look back and understand what had shaped us.

Through vulnerability you'll draw awareness to past events. You'll see them differently. You'll be able to honestly ask yourself, "These things that hurt me in my past, am I looking at them the way that I should, or am I framing them in a way that justifies wearing these masks and acting this way?"

You might talk to other people about those memories and find it feels good to trust people and to share. As you go deeper and experience more healing, even the way that you perceive painful memories, or the way you view memories of events that you know led to false manifestations of yourself, will change.

When I was young, everything was about performance because a good performance meant attention. I liked track and field because I could run fast. I remember running a race and someone exclaiming about how fast I ran and how much I liked the attention.

But since then the memory has been refreshed. Now I remember the smile on my face, and the joy and pleasure I felt in the running, rather than the time it took me to run or the attention I got.

This is a micro-healing — a reshaping of a memory that allows me to see the true purpose of that experience. As a child, I ran because it got me attention. Now I can see running for the pleasure it brings. There is no performance attached to it, no outside adulation that I need to receive in order to enjoy it. Now I can go running and have joy, not need.

That's the power of healing and forgiveness.

The Practice

Today and in the coming days, take some time in your ten-minute spot to remember the story of you and how the masks you're wearing came to be.

As memories and stories of your childhood rise to the surface, write them down and try to identify the connection between the stories of your past and the false actions of today.

This is not a time for recrimination or blame; it is a time for surrender and forgiveness.

> Don't dissect the past; you are a sum of all your experiences.
>
> Don't judge the past; accept where you are.
>
> Don't be afraid of what you will find; it will only be a version of you who needs forgiveness to be freed.

Forgiveness is the key that unchains you from the falsehoods so you can let them go and offer kindness and compassion. You'll experience healings and micro-healings as you remain open.

There may be pain, shame, embarrassment. When those emotions come up, practise saying,

> That was an older version of me, and I love her and accept her for who she was, but that's not who I am now.
>
> That was an earlier iteration of me, and I love him, and I thank him because he made the choices that led me to this place where I can embrace who I am now.
>
> I am grateful for my past because it led me to now.

I release any and all hope of a different past.

I am grateful for the joy of this moment and the hope of a future filled with all the potential that a forgiven me has.

Practice letting go of the past and the bitterness and the pain by loving yourself enough to say goodbye to the mistakes.

Release them and watch them flow from you, making space in your present moment for the hope of a future filled with a true expression of you.

Drop the mud of self-punishment and be free.

Hold on to the impossible and make it your possibility.

Give yourself the greatest gift.

Give yourself back to you.

STAGE III
Shine a Light of Awareness

"The darkness is our opportunity for enlightenment that leads us towards our truest potential."

John Stix

CHAPTER 6: AWAKEN TO PURPOSE

The Purpose-Driven Millennial

At our company offsite, we didn't fully define our company purpose and mission until the end of the day: "To deliver happiness and connections every day by being awesome." It still makes me laugh from a place of affection because it sounds so like us, and so completely unlike what you would expect to hear from a typical telecommunications company.

To us, our purpose means that we are going to strive ***to deliver happiness*** for our vendors, our customers, our community, our teammates, and ourselves. We deliver and support ***connection*** through data connections, voice connections, and interpersonal connection with our customers and each other. And ***being awesome*** means that we try to do and be our best each and every day, and if we can't be completely awesome one day, our teammates will be awesome by supporting us and helping to pick us up.

Shining a light of awareness on your purpose as a company is one of the most important aspects of what makes up a truly successful company. Companies, or the individuals within them, fail or give up or become lost for so many reasons, but I believe it's usually because of a disconnection with the purpose of the company. How can you have so many people in one organization be aligned if they've never defined what they're aligning on? A company purpose provides alignment for actions.

If a mantra is what binds you all together emotionally and keeps you facing in the same direction, the purpose is the roadmap to tell you what direction you're all heading in.

To discover our company purpose, we asked ourselves these questions:

> What is this business actually about?
>
> We spend a third of our lives devoted to a career and racing to fulfill our daily duties, but what are we really doing?
>
> What are we trying to accomplish?

We had forgotten those early days of being driven by the desire to be part of something, to learn, and to change even a small part of the world for the better. We had forgotten the thrill of achieving something as a group, of working together to generate change; that's a sensation that endures far beyond the fleeting satisfaction of a paycheque. And yet, so often, businesses forget the beginning and end up racing to get paid. But a business can't *just* be about the production of money.

To me, money is the byproduct of putting people and our dreams first; otherwise the early-days excitement gets lost in the day-to-day drudgery, and our motivation wanes, all because we forget the dreams of our very first day. A business needs to be more than just an operating company that turns a profit; it has to feel purposeful. A company purpose helps everyone remember foundational dreams, realize passion, and speak and act as if every day is the first day.

Millennials understand this sentiment, this need to align with purpose. I'm frequently asked, "John, how can I attract millennials to my company? How can I make them stay?"

I understand what they're asking. Gallup polls show that less than half of millennials polled plan to be at their current jobs one year from now, and 60% are willing to consider a different job opportunity. No wonder business owners are looking for ways to increase the motivation of their millennial employees.

From my perspective, millennials are easy to understand. I love this generation. They are pushing the envelope because they're looking for one thing and they won't settle until they find it: purpose. A paycheque isn't their primary motivation and they are deliberately constructing their lives so that they don't have to engage in the race of life just to acquire one at the expense of feeling personally fulfilled.

How many of us know what that's like?

So many of us get jobs based on the income they offer, and then we ramp up our lifestyle to match that pay and find ourselves trapped in a situation with no flexibility, placing all the control of our future in the hands of a company that doesn't care about our well-being.

Millennials are living together to reduce costs, stay mobile, and not get rooted. They don't want to find themselves in a position where they say, "I have to stay in a job that I hate because I have no savings" or "I can't chase my dreams because I have an expensive life to live. I have no idea what other passions I have and even if I did, how would I pursue them when I'm working ten hours a day for someone else?"

If you want to attract millennials, you need to first discover your WHO as a leader, and then the WHO of your business to find your company's purpose and align others with this purpose. Then tell the world and wait for the attraction to begin. My answer is: they will come to you!

Attraction and alignment in both our corporate and personal lives always happen when we're living from our heart, aligning our inner WHO with our outer actions. It might come in little bits and pieces, with the faint ringing of a phone now and then. But as you answer the call, imagine all that your life can be, and take small steps towards your dream, you'll awaken to your true purpose and potential.

Awakening

It's easy to identify others who have answered the call and awoken to purpose. A while back, I was watching ***America's Got Talent***. A thirteen-year-old girl comes out on stage. The judges ask her what courses she likes in school.

"Music."

"What kind of music?"

A shrug and a giggle. "I don't know."

She's on stage. She's palpably nervous. The judges are telling her it's OK to be nervous, but, "You're here for a reason. Go for it." The audience is wondering if the fear is going to win. And then she starts to sing.

Go watch it. Even if you've seen it before, I challenge you to search right now for "Courtney Hadwin *America's Got Talent* audition" and watch her sing. Watch her come alive on stage. Watch her be completely connected to what she's doing to the point where a nervous young girl transforms into a fiery, passionate, heart-centred individual whose every fibre, every hair on her head, every nerve ending in her body is vibrating with an electricity powered by her dreams.

From my perspective, this is someone whose dreams are perfectly aligned with her behaviour. This is someone who has awoken to purpose. This is living inward in action.

She doesn't need to explain to us, the judges, or even to herself why she loves music or what she loves about it. She can't even put it into words when the judges ask her. And it doesn't matter. We don't need to have her say, "When I sing, I feel alive. When I sing, I feel joyful. When I sing, I feel like I'm doing exactly what I'm supposed to be doing. When I sing, everything else fades away and I'm completely present in the moment."

You don't even have to love her style of singing. You may not like the song she sings, or the way she moves on stage, or the sound of her voice. But I defy you to deny that she is singing from her heart, that her actions are being driven by her seeds of purpose, that her singing is a soul expression, and that she is outwardly expressing the truth of what she has found within.

It doesn't mean it's easy. Presumably she didn't wake up that morning and decide to audition, having never before sung a note. I imagine that behind her performance is years of training and growth and pain. She doubtless had to learn how to endure and forgive criticism from herself and others. It must have been hard for her to get up there on the stage of her life, literally and figuratively, and sing in front of all of those people and be judged.

I know first-hand that being authentic and vulnerable in front of people is hard, no matter how connected you are to what you're doing — in fact, the more authentic you are the harder it can be.

Being connected doesn't mean there's no work involved, and often the work is challenging, but it's also effortless because you know it's so exactly what you're supposed to be doing, and that a life lived without it wouldn't be a life at all.

That's how I feel when I go onstage to speak or when I'm mediating at another company's offsite. In that moment right before I open my mouth to speak, I'm battling nervousness and anxiety. The fear is getting at me, trying to hold me back. Then I take a deep breath and I feel the excitement of the moment. My senses lift, I'm acutely aware of everything around me, and a joy spreads through me as I realize I'm not just randomly helping people but actually serving them and living my purpose. It's a feeling of all my dreams coming true in one gigantic rush that encompasses me, and I wish everyone could feel this way.

Do you know these moments?

If a life bomb is that moment when everything seems to shatter and you feel completely alone, this moment is the exact opposite. It's a moment when you feel like everything has just slowed right down, and your inner WHO and your outer actions are perfectly aligned. You feel a deep, purposeful connection to everything around you, knowing that you are exactly where you should be.

You have goosebumps
    you feel joy
        you feel peaceful
            and you have a huge smile on your face

You might experience it during your workday
or when you're with your partner, walking hand in
hand down the street
or playing with your children
or sitting reading a book
or walking your dog

These moments are individual to every person, and they will come, not just when we're up on stage singing but when we're by ourselves or with people we love; anytime we are engaging in activities that are aligned with our WHO.

> Do we live for those moments or do we live within those moments?
>
> How do we immerse ourselves within these moments?
>
> Isn't this what we truly dream and wish for in our lives — these moments of pure joy and purpose being fulfilled in everything that we do?
>
> Isn't this why we exist, and not just exist but actually live?

But how do we have more and more of them, time and time again?

It starts by picking up the phone when your authentic self calls and delivers a message about the dreams of your heart.

Then you take a tiny step towards that dream, whether it's by telling someone about it or by just getting started on one small aspect — baking one loaf of bread or calling up an old friend, whatever it is that your intuition says needs to happen to move you closer to the dream you can imagine.

If imagination is the lens giving you a view of your dream, intuition is the compass that will guide you to that dream.

Follow that intuition and take a small step towards what you can envision. Pay attention to how you feel throughout these small steps and where these moments lead you. Those feelings and moments will shine a light of awareness on what is important to you. They are another phone ringing in your life, and when you answer the call, these moments unleash potential and hidden gifts as you awaken to your true purpose.

Vancouver was an experience of awakening for me. I had gone there with a dream to start understanding myself, to seek my own identity. And I made a commitment to listen for the phones ringing in my life, to take small steps towards that dream.

At the end of a long and unusual day, when I had listened to my intuition and followed a winding path through the city, ending up at English Bay, I had picked up the phone when I heard it ringing and telling me I had something to say. I opened my mouth and out of it came that poem. It was a moment of discovering a gift that I didn't know I had and listening to ideas buried deep within me that I didn't know were there.

When I got home from Vancouver, I couldn't stop writing. It felt like I was reaching into my soul and pulling out words and thoughts I'd never even considered before. Ideas and philosophies about caring for myself and others, theories about forgiveness and love — they all came pouring out of my pen, making me wonder where it was all coming from. Why were these thoughts and theories in me? Where had they been hidden all this time?

While I was writing, I would experience excitement, joy, shivers, goosebumps — an unfamiliar feeling of being perfectly connected to my purpose, even if I didn't have a clear view yet of what that purpose was or where it was going to lead.

Going to my ten-minute spot every day to write out these thoughts and feelings emboldened me to speak to people around me about the seed of care I had found. Sharing my thoughts and feelings with people in my life and workplace led to huge changes in our workplace, which led to opportunities for me to speak to other business leaders about the process we went through. Immersing myself in these moments of purpose and taking the small steps my heart was telling me take, led me to a moment in Las Vegas where everything finally culminated in a perfect alignment of what I believe about workplace culture and the purpose I had awoken to in my heart.

Put Your Headphones On

It was my biggest speech yet, delivering the keynote address to close out Impact 15, in Las Vegas. Impact 15 is North America's largest internet marketing conference, attracting leaders from all over the United States and Canada, and I had been asked to give a talk about workplace culture.

I had been speaking publicly for only about eight months. While outwardly, I may have appeared confident, the speed and quick scaling of this new part of my life was causing me some serious internal insecurity. But the same speed and seeming acceptance of the message I was trying to spread made the prospect of talking in front of such an august group intoxicating. Fear mixed with exhilaration is a heady cocktail. I had goosebumps all over and a heightened sense of being totally alive.

If I close my eyes, I can still recall minute details about that day. Huge chandeliers hung from the ceiling of an intimidatingly large room. A cream-coloured design wandered through the red carpet. I was wearing my I'M IN T-shirt and pacing up and down the hallway outside the room, awaiting my turn. My hands were sweating, and the anxiety had wiped my memory; no matter how hard I tried, I couldn't remember the opening part of my speech. Hoping to centre myself, I put on my headphones and listened to the sound track of a motivational video.

The funny thing about those headphones was that they prevented me from hearing the end of the speech by the speaker who came before me, a person of authority who was downplaying the importance and lasting significance of corporate culture. I found out afterwards that he spoke out against almost everything I had planned to say.

Fortunately, I didn't know that as I got up on stage. Standing there, looking out over the audience, I realized how far I had come in such a short span of time, and how blessed I was to have found my passion for helping people become the best possible version of themselves. The thought of not spreading my message was worse than the anxiety, and a sense of mindful calm moved through me. Any fear I'd had was overwritten by the excitement of being my true self and following my dreams, and I was left with a deep sense of purpose to share what was in my heart.

On that stage, I told everyone my true message of being authentic, of being open, of being vulnerable. I told them that it is by diving deep that we learn who we are, and that by knowing ourselves we learn how to be the best leader, best parent, best partner, or best friend that we can be.

I told them that my wish for all leaders is for them to look inward and ask themselves, "What can I do to take care of the authentic me? What is holding me back from embracing the true warmth and kindness inside so that I can share it with everyone under my care?"

Somewhere along the way, companies fell in love with profits and retained earnings, more than with leading people and creating communities. In so many businesses, we have replaced the identity of our teammates with numbers on file folders shoved away in cold, grey filing cabinets or stored on someone's computer within Human Resources.

Company leaders used to shake the hands of their employees in the morning, welcoming back their second family to work each day. We used to care about what was happening in our teammates' lives and we invested in our community because success was about the people, not the bottom line. Too many company leaders have stripped away the care and replaced it with statements like, "Don't take it personally; it's just business" or "While you're here at work you will work. Period. When you're at home, then you can have fun" or "Leave your personal life at home." Those sentiments are completely unnatural — of course our personal lives are going to impact our work lives and the other way around.

> Why can't we empower our staff to have it all?
>
> Why can't we as leaders realize that then we, in turn, can also have it all?
>
> Doesn't it make sense that a happy and well cared–for workforce would be more productive?

Leaders at all levels want to feel a connection and a sense of belonging, but too many of them closet themselves away in their offices, shutting themselves off from those they are most responsible for. As a result, they lose touch with their people and their business.

That day, I shared my belief that business leaders can choose a better way to treat the people in our care. I believe we can create significant shareholder value, company revenue, growth, and company retention, while deeply caring and showing care for our teammates.

I shared my belief that taking a business through a deep cultural diagnosis and healing process produces an explosion of company-wide conviction and a culture of legitimate passion.

I shared my belief that it's not a weakness to open your heart and be vulnerable; it's a strength that fosters connection and growth.

My message was simple, and I left them with a question to consider: Why is it so scary to be open and vulnerable, to embrace employees as teammates, to treat them with compassion and support their dreams?

That speech was a significant turning point for me. I shared more than I ever had before about the emotion behind my theories and practices, and I walked off stage, leaving behind me any fear of ever sharing it again. I had found my true purpose and a deep sense of loving myself. I fell in love, not with speaking but with the message and with the feeling we all experienced together in that room, the feeling of everyone leaning in and connecting to the message and to each other. It came from a true expression of the seeds of purpose that I had found when I began living inward, and it reaffirmed in my heart that I am connected to that purpose.

Afterwards, the chairman and founder of the Internet Marketing Association approached me and told me that in the twelve years the event had been running, my speech was the first one to receive a standing ovation. This was yet another amazing confirmation that I was doing exactly what I was called to do. And it was amusing, considering the speaker before me had had nothing good to say about corporate culture. But because I'd had my headphones on, I didn't hear my detractor. Instead, I was listening to the seeds of purpose in my heart.

The next time you're about to embark on fulfilling your dream or any action you KNOW is connected to your purpose, realize and understand that there will always be detractors.

There will be people and events that come against you. But just put your headphones on and do it anyway. Because when you're done, there will be someone standing for you.

PRACTICE: The One-Minute Spot

Background

The purpose of any kind of practice in our lives is for us to improve, get stronger, get better, and become more skillful, and often we also get faster. As I practised going daily to my ten-minute spot, I found that my ten-minute spot turned into one-minute spots that I could have anytime during the day.

The one-minute spot is a brief moment of self-care that you can experience anywhere. It's a way to carry with you the sense of peace that you've found in your ten-minute spot and a way to constantly reconnect back to your dream.

When I went to Vancouver, I took with me a dream of what I wanted to accomplish. I wanted to dive deep into understanding who I was, and I was committed to listening to the phones ringing to tell me when I was on the right path. I didn't set aside a particular time of day to do this; I was open to it the entire time I was there. I had a snapshot of a dream in my head — a dream to seek my true self — and I carried that snapshot with me at all times, referring to it constantly throughout the day, checking in everywhere I went and in every action I took, to make sure that what I was doing was moving me in the direction of that dream.

Part of the commitment of answering the phone is having faith and being willing to commit to the adventure, even if you don't know what you're going to do or what it's going to look like. It's about making a conscious decision to engage with the adventure and listen to your authentic self on the other end of the phone and then watch the path open up before you. It can happen at any time of the day, and the one-minute spot is a way of remaining open all day to following that path.

The Practice

Up until now, you've been going actively to your ten-minute spot; it's time to start bringing a piece of your ten-minute spot with you and turning it into a one-minute spot, by taking a snapshot of the dream you want to accomplish and then consulting that snapshot throughout the day.

Remember: imagination is what shows you your dreams. Intuition will point you to the seeds of purpose and give you a compass to follow so you can start chasing your dreams. Taking a small step in the direction of your dreams will lead to potential and purpose fulfilled.

Today in your ten-minute spot, close your eyes and clearly envision the dream that you wish for your life.

> Is it to start finding fulfillment in your work life by baking bread?
>
> Is it to renew old friendships by playing tennis?

Is it to write a book?
sing a song?
give a speech?

You know what your dream is; picture it clearly in your head, with as much detail as you can.

Where are you?

Who are you with?

What are you doing?

How do you feel?

Take a mental snapshot of it. If you want, draw a picture of it or write some keywords that will instantly bring the picture to mind.

Now you can start to practise consulting the snapshot you carry in your head, in one-minute spots throughout the day. Look at the snapshot when you wake up in the morning, while you're going to work, while you're in a meeting, while you're having lunch with a friend, while you're sitting with your partner, or when you're playing with your kids.

Each time you consult the snapshot, consult your intuition and ask what small step you could take in that moment that you know is connected to your purpose.

In any moment, you can ask yourself:

> Is this action moving me closer to my dream, and is the way I'm attempting to accomplish it a true expression of the true me?
>
> Am I embracing love, joy, empathy, compassion, kindness, forgiveness?
>
> Am I approaching this situation with a seed of care and an attitude of heart-centredness?
>
> Am I taking an account of my abilities and letting fear be only the passenger?
>
> Am I being my own hero of my journey, honouring myself and others through my actions while expressing care to myself?

In the one-minute spot, look for the light of awareness that will clearly illuminate the path your heart has put before you, and ask yourself what step you can take that will move you along that path. And then take that step.

> Fear will enter in. Remember, it's a liar and you can let it be the passenger.
>
> Detractors will try to pull you away. Put your headphones on and do it anyway.

Don't let anything stand between you and your true purpose.

CHAPTER 7: PAUSE AND EMBRACE A GROWTH MINDSET

Reframe the Negativity

For a time after we made huge internal changes in our company, I had a lot of success being hired to speak about workplace culture at marketing and human resource events and to individual corporations. They would book me for four or five talks a month, all across Canada and the United States. And then, seemingly out of the blue, the bookings stopped. It made me anxious and made me question everything.

> Why am I not getting any more talks?
>
> What's going on?

When I stopped being anxious, I realized that what seemed like a setback was actually a need for a pause. I had to learn something new, be refreshed by investing in self-care and nourishment, and find balance in other areas of my life before the talks could start again.

That's how it will go on the living inward journey:

> Progress
>
> Pause
>
> Lesson
>
> Heal
>
> Pause
>
> Progress

It's a trajectory that's not always moving up, always experiencing growth — healing and growth will come more often during times of rest. Rather, it's a pattern of micro-steps and micro-growth and micro-healings, within and between the stages. If everything appears to be slowing down, or your growth seems to be stopping, ask yourself these questions:

> Am I in a pause state?
>
> Is there something here for me to learn and grow from?
>
> Do I need to take a moment without judgement to reflect, to surrender, to check the compass?

Living inward is about growing holistically. When you appear to stop growing, you have to learn why. Embrace the fundamentals of

openness
self-acceptance
vulnerability
forgiveness
kindness
compassion

Then ask yourself:

What is blocking me?

What is stopping me from progression?

What is stopping me from moving down the path that is leading me to my better self?

When you pause, you can take time to observe and learn before moving forward again.

It's about reframing what you think is a negative and seeing how it is leading you to something better by embracing a growth mindset.

Polar opposites in life are all around us. So often we see an experience as positive or negative, and the way in which that experience shapes us depends on our point of view.

Imagine yourself going for a walk along a beautiful tree-lined path. When are you more likely to stop and admire one of the trees? When are you more likely to think of that tree as being in a growth state?

> In spring when the tree is in bloom?
>
> In summer when the tree is covered in fruit?
>
> In fall when the leaves are turning bright yellow and orange?
>
> Or in winter, when the branches are bare and stark against a grey sky?

In all four seasons, it's still the same tree, but your perception of when it looks healthy, beautiful, and growing, is subjective, based on the season and your point of view. But even in winter, when it looks as if all growth has stopped, the roots continue to grow. Even when the ground freezes solid, growth is only temporarily halted, and the tree rests, until the season passes, spring returns, and growth resumes.

Throughout winter, it's the same healthy, beautiful tree, just in a different season, and it will bloom with fresh leaves once again. Just like you are, and you will. Recently I heard someone say, "We are not ***going*** through it, we are ***growing*** through it."

Embracing a growth mindset is less about handling the

negative and more about reframing it and looking at it from another viewpoint. It helps you to see that the majority of situations that you think are negative are not happening *to* you, but *for* you.

Because there is something to learn from them.

There is growth that will come from them.

You need to progress through them so that you can embrace the wisdom that lies within them, and learn that growth is still ongoing, even when it appears to have stopped.

So often when we're going through times of setback and suffering, we think, ***No one gets me. No one could possibly understand what I'm going through. I'm alone in all of this.***

The thought, ***I am alone*** is a lie that needs to be reframed. There are more than seven billion people on this planet. Why do we feel so alone?

Is it even possible that you're the only person to have ever felt what you're feeling?

Realizing that you're not alone takes the edge off. It takes away that feeling of isolation that is part of the pain. It reframes the pain and allows you to see the picture differently.

Reframing is about remembering that while we're going through a time of suffering or setback, we can have faith that we will get through it. It's about seeing this moment as a storm in our lives and making the decision that this will be a season, not a lifetime.

During each storm, decide to use it as an opportunity for learning.

> What can I learn from this?
>
> How can I grow?
>
> How will this change me for the better once I pass through it?
>
> And how will going through this storm allow me to help someone going through a similar storm in the future to feel less alone?

I've watched people go through life bombs that completely destroy every seemingly good thing in their life. They move through the stages of grief and anger and then comes the time to make a decision. Some of them decide to start moving on; they see the life bomb as a storm they move through to the next phase. But others stay in the storm for far longer than they should. They say, "I'll never recover from this. All the best parts of my life are behind me," and they stay mired in depression and anxiety.

When a storm has taken hold of you to the point where you feel like you can never move through it — where you feel stuck — it can help to reframe the negativity. Realize and embrace the truth that, in any moment, you can be happy, joyful, content.

It could happen in the very next moment if you're open to it. Contentment comes when you are connected to your WHO, and you can experience contentment even during suffering.

Joy happens when you're being authentic in your purpose and your dreams. Happiness and joy are a choice, but you must be open to receive them. Even in storms, you can find something to be grateful for and find a place of contentment. Even in storms, you can dream.

Being open to contentment, being open to what this storm can teach you, means you've embraced a growth mindset. As children, our whole existence is a growth mindset. Everything we do is about growing physically and mentally.

As parents, every day is about nurturing our children to grow. We hope that they grow in knowledge — that's why we send them to school. We hope they grow in faith — that's why we share our beliefs with them and take them to church or synagogue or mosque. We encourage them in their social experiences because we want them to grow as part of a community.

But are we, as adults, continuing to grow?

How many of us, when we hit a certain age, think we're finished? We say, "Yup, that's done. I'm an adult now. I'm done with growing."

No! A growth mindset is about realizing that we should never stop growing. It's about constantly looking inward to remember your identity, to discover what matters to you as an individual, to discover what is connected to your purpose and then embrace life and keep moving through it.

It's your birthright to grow and to stay on the path of growing. A growth mindset will allow you to see that what appears as a threat is really a challenge — something to overcome to get you closer to your dreams.

Fear will always step into this process. Fear says, "That thing you did before? Yeah, it wasn't that great. You couldn't do that again. No way, that won't work."

It's always there. But remember, fear's appearance confirms that you're on the right path and that you're about to experience growth and a breakthrough. That's the cost of growth — continually being pulled back as you're progressing to the next level.

It's physiologically sound. As children progress through stages of growth, they will regress in their behaviour before they progress. As they approach learning to walk, suddenly behaviours they had mastered start to fall apart — they may stop eating as well or sleeping as well, until they get walking under control and then everything settles down again.

Similarly, before you can progress, often you will regress in the form of fear, or doubt, or anxiety, or situations that appear to be holding you back, or getting in the way and creating distraction and interference. With each phase, and with each step towards your dreams, there will be hooks and setbacks among the successes.

So what do you do with them? You reframe them.

You understand that they are part of the process but that they should never stop you from growing as a person; they should never be allowed to distract you or move you further from your dreams and, in fact, they can contribute to your growth.

But sometimes you will need to step back and change your point of view. You will need to pause, see what you can learn, embrace a growth mindset, and invest in yourself with self-nourishment and care.

Invest in Self-Nourishment and Care

When we were going through all the changes in our workplace, I was so enthralled with being my true self at work that I lost all thought of what balance in my life should look like. I couldn't stop thinking about workplace culture and about the company. Even when I wasn't physically at the office, mentally I was engaged with it. After my realization in Vancouver about how much I love people, back in the office I was dropping everything to go and help anyone who needed me, thinking that was the best way to show my love and care for them. I thought that by emptying myself out for people, I was loving them, forgetting all about the principle of keeping my own cup full. In failing to love and care for myself, and in pursuing my dreams in only one area of my life, I burned out. I needed to get away.

I found a beautiful retreat in Arizona dedicated to providing space and time for awakening and recovery. It was a place of restoration where I learned that I didn't need to rush through the stages — that even though I was excited about everything I was discovering about myself, and excited to share myself with everyone, I still needed to take time for healing.

I realized that if I was going to drop everything to help someone, it had to be for the right reason and not just to prop them up so I could feel their affection. I did it so innocently, and yet it was still a trap — detrimental to the person I was trying to help and to myself. Taking the time to nourish myself was so necessary for growth, healing, and perspective.

Looking inside to listen to your heart, discovering your WHO, discovering your dreams, and realizing there can be more to your life than you're currently experiencing, can make you want to rush ahead and embrace this new awareness. Part of being the hero of your journey is to remember not to pour all your energy into your dream to the detriment of your own health and well-being.

It can be overwhelming when you first start to really think

about what matters to you and entertain the possibility of having it in your life. You're freeing your dreams and starting to live a life that is in line with your authentic self. You start to awaken to purpose, which creates a lot of energy and excitement. But being on the right path doesn't mean you should run down it as quickly as you can.

Naturally, if you've been wandering down a path in life that isn't filled with authentic purpose, suddenly finding yourself heading in a new direction will be exhilarating. This makes self-care and self-nourishment even more important. A friend of mine compares it to being lost while you're out driving in your car. You consult the map and finally figure out where you are and how to get where you're going, but that doesn't mean you should race down the road at your car's top speed. You still need to be safe; you still need to arrive in one piece. Self-nourishment and care will keep you centred and balanced and healthy.

Your heart will remind you of the things you used to do that brought you joy, activities that brought you a feeling of care. It could be something as simple as, I used to go to the market every weekend. It made me feel great. I loved going to the market and while I was there, I would buy a coffee and walk around and talk to people and pick up flowers for my wife and buy fresh foods and, and, and.... As soon as your heart speaks to you, it starts to cascade and you think, ***Oh yeah... why did I stop doing that? Why did I just put that aside?***

Listen to the still small voice of your heart that says, ***It would*** *be nice to go the market again.* Why did I stop?

I stopped because I'm always putting everything else ahead of myself. I'm always sacrificing what matters to me as an individual and getting involved in things that don't matter as much.

Maybe you replaced going to the market with cutting the lawn because it was something that had to be done. I'm not saying there aren't things that have to be done, but where does that end?

When did you start erasing yourself to the point where you're never doing the things that matter to you?

Carving out time for self-nourishment starts with you and it's what allows you to flourish and fill your cup. It allows you to do the things you love and then it flows out to others and allows you to care for them. It gives you time to get used to this new path you're on, or even still just heading towards.

An investment of self-nourishment will look different for each person. This is another opportunity to return to your ten-minute spot and use your memory and imagination to find what is nourishing for you. Or even to use your one-minute spot so that in any particular moment you can ask yourself if a particular action is self-nourishing, or if it's going to take more from you than you have to give in this moment, or if you're wanting to give it for the wrong reasons.

> You may naturally gravitate towards yoga or going to the gym.
>
> Maybe there's a hobby you always wanted to pursue.
>
> Maybe you always wanted a dog to take for walks.
>
> Maybe you don't instinctively know what you need.

Ask yourself what it looks like to live this new life of chasing your dream, still nourishing and taking care of yourself.

You deserve self-love. We all do. I think it is one of the most important and one of the most frequently missing "secret ingredients" of a joyful, purposeful life. Often we're simply lacking the self-nourishment and self-care that we all deserve to experience. We're so quick to be busy, racing somewhere, pleasing others. It's a beautiful thing to help others, but too seldom do we take the time to nourish ourselves, to express love to ourselves, and to enjoy who we are.

As you progress through the steps of the inward journey you'll find out how important it is to

find space in your life to love yourself
treat yourself respectfully
believe that your dreams are important
know that your voice being heard is important
and look at yourself with acceptance and love

Do it right now and try to remember to do it every single day.

PRACTICE: Pause and Express Gratitude for Now

Background

Pauses are necessary for growth. Kids get growing pains at night because they grow while they're asleep. What do we say to someone when they're unwell? "Get some rest." Rest, stillness, and pausing, rather than frenetic constant movement, are aligned with healing and growth.

If you feel you've been on a steady trajectory of growth and are now finding resistance, hooks, and setbacks, take some time to pause.

> Invest in self-nourishment and care.
>
> Stop moving.
>
> Be still.

Look around and see what there is to learn from this time of rest and what you can incorporate into your life that will bring you refreshment. Use this time to reframe what you might think of as negativity and practice gratitude instead.

When you're focusing on something that seems to be in the way, a roadblock or setback, it can be easy to forget just how far you've already come. Gratitude is a powerful emotion to embrace during a pause, to look back and see what you've already accomplished, how much closer you are to achieving your dreams, how much of your WHO you've been able to discover and realize.

The Practice

Try to practise gratitude and be grateful for even the small things in your life. Gratitude will keep you in this present moment rather than looking forward with anxiety or looking back with regret. When you practice gratitude, you are firmly rooted in the now.

What are you grateful for right now, in this moment, with no thoughts or worries of what tomorrow will bring, with no thoughts about the problems that need solving or the stress that is in your life?

> Are you grateful for health? Maybe you struggle with chronic pain but in this moment you're free from pain.
>
> Are you grateful for people in your life?
>
> For your home?
>
> A beautiful sunset?

Find something, even one small thing, that brings you pleasure in this moment and about which you can express gratitude.

List as many things, big or small, for which you are grateful.

List as many areas of your life as you can in which you know you've experienced growth, even if that growth appears to be slowing down.

Think and write about how it feels to experience that sense of gratitude and that contentment that comes from knowing that you are starting to live a life that is more in line with your WHO.

Hold onto that feeling and carry it with you throughout your day so that at any moment you can find that emotion and experience joy and contentment, even in times of challenge and hardship.

CHAPTER 8: YOUR HEART IS YOUR ORIGIN

Live Your Mantra

After the offsite, I spent the weekend looking forward to Monday, knowing the team would have so many thoughts and ideas to share about what we had been through. I suspected that most of the leaders wouldn't wait until Monday, and sure enough, comments and questions were soon pouring into my email. A feeling of joy grew in my heart as I read the authentic exchange of dialogue, and I longed for a way to preserve and maintain all the care and excitement the team was expressing.

I wondered about finding a mantra, a short phrase that would encapsulate these emotions and bind us all together. I had read about companies defining values, purpose, mission, and vision as part of their workplace culture development, but I had never heard of a company with a corporate mantra, and I believed it would make the identity of our business come alive.

One afternoon, at the end of a workday, several of us spontaneously gathered outside a co-worker's office and tossed around ideas of what our mantra could be. We agreed that we wanted a phrase that would bind us all together as a team, beyond our core values. We wanted a phrase to keep us focused on our intention to grow a culture of inclusion while honouring our entrepreneurial history.

People always loved the "out of the basement of a house" David and Goliath story of us taking on the giant phone and internet companies. At the beginning, the magnitude of what we were trying to do had seemed insurmountable. My co-founders and I had had no money to speak of. We lived off of microwave dinners and macaroni and cheese. We shared a single pair of dress shoes and a blazer, taking it in turns to wear them to meetings. Through it all, what pushed us forward wasn't the thought of the fancy cars we might one day drive, or the idea of the big houses we might one day buy. It was our common dream to challenge the status quo, to really make a difference. We had so little, but there was no question we were all "in."

That was it.

I'M IN.

It said so much with so little:

> I'm in to being happy.
>
> I'm in to succeeding.
>
> I'm in to embracing the purpose and values of this amazing company.

We agreed that I'M IN would be our mantra, knowing it would say all the right things to our teammates and our future hires.

I can't tell you what a difference it has made in our business to have this mantra or stress how important it is to have an emotional bond that all of your teammates share within your organization. A mantra tells you that you're all beating from the same drum — that you've each signed up to be a part of what you're collectively trying to achieve.

In all the speaking I've ever done, an emotional bond has consistently been at the core of every successful organization I've ever looked at. You can have a fantastic product, slick marketing, and a powerful strategy, but without a belief system that represents what your organization is all about, you will have individuals and groups within the business who are not pulling together simply because they are not engaged with the purpose.

I'M IN is still our personal statement towards each other, and we are all so proud that with two small words we can express all that we are. I'M IN!

I frequently say that corporate culture is not a one-day event. Yes, we spent a day off site, figuring out who we were as a company and then another day defining our mantra. But it's an everyday process to say our mantra and to live it. It's an everyday process to embrace our core values of trust, accountability, "just do it and find a solution," innovation, teamwork, and happiness (including happiness of mind, body, and spirit).

In every action we take, be it in our sales campaigns, marketing strategies, internal operations, or communications with customers and teammates, we strive to reflect our core values and live out our mantra. They are the foundation of our company and they reflect who we are. They provide focus and they drive every decision we make so that our inner WHO is aligned with our outward actions.

Similarly, as you're acting on the seed of care you've found within yourself and expressing the things that matter to you, you're being directed by your core values. As you peel back the masks and discover more of who you are and what your dreams are, you'll discover the guideposts that you want to live your life by; these core values reflect who you are at a fundamental level and they will be the framework for how you make decisions, how you honour yourself, and how you honour everyone you come in contact with.

Mantras that you discover within yourself are what keep you focused and grounded. They encapsulate your core values, speaking directly to you, reminding you of who you are and what you're seeking.

The daily "Who Am I?" practice will help you develop your personal mantra, something you can say to keep yourself focused on who you are, and keep you open to discovering more.

A mantra will remind you to embrace knowledge

wisdom
authority
and purposeful acceptance

It will remind you to accept who and where you are today, but to always be thirsty for more, to always peel back more of the mask to discover and release more of your WHO.

It will remind you to not stay trapped by the false ego.

The more you stay trapped today, the more you rob yourself of tomorrow's joy.

Your mantra can be a simple message of acceptance:

> I accept who I am and where I am in each moment. I am on a path of discovery and growth. I do not hinder myself with self-doubt and judgement. I remain in a present state of acceptance of me.

Your mantra can be one of seeking:

> I am working towards bettering myself and making decisions that honour who I am. I am seeking and gaining wisdom and knowledge that informs my growth. I am seeking self-love and self-improvement by doing a little every day without judgement or expectation.

I encourage everyone to develop a mantra that works for them and say it every day. Mantras are fluid and as you go through your inward journey, your mantra will change to align more and more closely with your core values and your authentic self. You'll know when it is time to change your mantra when it is no longer in line with who you are.

Your mantra points you towards your core values, and your core values guide how you live out your life as an expression of your WHO.

> But where do your core values live?
>
> Where can you go to find your mantra and learn how to express it?
>
> What fuels your soul expression and is at the very core of the authentic you?

All the answers are there when you let your heart be the origin of your life.

Your heart is where everything begins.

Listen to Your Heart and Have Faith

In the earliest stages of your development, your heart was the first organ to form, enabling a tiny collection of cells to efficiently work together.

It enabled life.

It's your origin.

What's the point on a grid called where the X and Y axes intersect?

That's the origin.

It's the starting point for that system, where the grid snaps together and from where everything is measured.

The origin creates alignment.

Think of the X and Y axes of your body. The vertical axis starts at the top of your head and goes down through your heart and the rest of your body.

Extend your arms out to either side of yourself. Your horizontal axis starts at the tips of your fingers on one hand, passes through your heart and ends at the tips of your fingers on your other hand.

On the vertical axis is your head and your thoughts.

On the horizontal axis are your hands, your actions, what you're touching and doing in life.

The intersection of these axes is your heart. Your heart is in line with your head to direct your thoughts and in line with your hands to direct to your actions.

It is your heart that ensures balance and alignment.

The living inward journey is about finding alignment in your life between your heart, your head, and your actions, so that you can live out your purpose.

You will miss the true power of your life's purpose if you do not align your outward actions with your inward journey.

In listening to your heart and honouring what you've discovered there, your outward actions will be driven by your core values. It is your heart that will tell you how to

honour yourself
honour others
chase your dreams
actively live your mantra in a way that is true to who you are

Up to this point, you've spent time in your ten-minute spot, remembering dreams of youth, remembering how to dream.

You've looked back and embraced healing.

You've looked deep inside to find who you truly are and as you've put faith in the dream and started to take small steps towards it, you're getting a taste of what a true expression of yourself can be in a specific area of your life.

Maybe you started with your career as you remembered a love of baking bread, or you focused on friendships and wanting to play tennis again.

Maybe you have a dream to:

design a new logo for your company
open a flower shop
be a nurse
be a farmer

As you pursue the dream, in whatever small way you can, you will start to express more of who you are, and it will feel amazing.

You'll receive encouragement.

You'll become more creative, more joyful.

You'll see the ripple effect around you as you spark creativity and joy in others.

But at some point, you will come up against challenges, against people who don't support what you're doing, against situations that discourage you or set you back. This is where your core values and mantras will guide you through these challenges.

What does that look like?

Let's say that you have a mantra to stay true to yourself, and two of your core values are to remain in love with your partner and to embrace and spread joy. You've been baking bread every day, and you love it; you jump out of bed every morning at 4:30 to bake bread before you go to work, filled with joy because you love doing it and you love feeding your family, friends, and co-workers every morning with fresh bread.

You decide you want to open a store and you express that dream to your partner. They may fully support you in that dream, but admittedly their reaction may not be everything you've hoped for. They may argue that your dream is not realistic or achievable.

It is your mantra and your values that will guide you and help you treat this slice of your life with the same value system that you used to start baking bread in the first place. Here is where you can also use your one-minute spot to consult your heart and let your mantra and values sustain you to stay true to what is at the core of your dream and the joy it brings, while honouring your partner and engaging in the discussion from a place of love.

Don't let any toxic emotions dictate your behaviour — take any anger and put it aside; anger is what we resort to, to cover up fear or sadness, and it will never get you to the root of the issue.

Don't be defensive — the need to defend yourself actually comes from not knowing your WHO.

Instead, get to the heart of what your partner is saying to you; find the core of their reaction:

> Are they feeling insecure about what you're expressing, not knowing what the reality of your dream will mean for the financial security of the family?
>
> Are they feeling that you following your dream is taking you away from them, as you're spending more and more time pursuing your dream, forgoing important family time?
>
> Are they feeling resentful because they have dreams of their own that they want to follow?

You need to address these feelings while you honour your values and act in a way that is true to what you've found deep inside. When you have peace and faith in who you are and what life holds for you, you eliminate the need to defend yourself, and you become more positive in your thoughts and more hopeful about what the future holds.

If fear is our passenger, hope is the highway ahead.

Hope is shaped by knowing your WHO, by having faith that your mantra and your core values are true to you and that you can rely on your heart to make the right decisions.

Hope insulates you from the distractions, the roadblocks, and the problems that you need to overcome. It insulates you because you can have faith that if what you're doing is in line with your core values, the ripple effect will be so much greater and more positive than anything you have to be afraid of.

If baking bread is bringing you joy, and you know that opening a shop is going to bring you more joy, that joy will spread to your partner, your family, your friends, and your customers. The effect of living your core value of embracing and spreading joy in your life and in the lives of those around you will bring alignment with customers who love your bread and your joy. The ripple effect of living the soul expression of your mantra and your core values on a daily basis is immeasurable.

That doesn't mean you should put your family in financial distress or create a rift between you and your partner or your friends to pursue your dream. If your core value is to remain in love with your partner and spread joy, then you need to find a way to live your dream and be true to yourself, while still honouring your partner. It will not bring your partner joy for you to ignore their concerns.

You need to seek alignment.

Don't allow yourself to be derailed just because you can't completely give up your career and your salary right now. You've found a path that is making sense and resonates and creates excitement in your heart. But you have to treat every aspect of your life like that, even the people who might have trouble with what you're doing.

Ask yourself how you can honour them and still honour what you've discovered about yourself.

Have faith that your soul expression can honour you both.

Have faith that you're going in the right direction because your heart has confirmed it.

A while back, I was on a business trip to attend a meeting that I felt was really important for my journey. After calling for a cab to pick me up from the hotel, I went to get my wallet out of the room's safe but it wouldn't open. I called downstairs and someone came up to help. He tried everything but couldn't get it open either. By this point, the cab had arrived and was waiting for me downstairs. I was running late for my meeting and starting to get anxious.

Finally the hotel staff managed to get the safe open and I ran downstairs to the ATM to get cash for the cab. But the ATM wasn't working either. I apologized to the cab driver for being late and asked him if we could stop at a bank machine along the way.

"It'll be an extra $20.00 for stopping," he said.

I almost threw my hands up in the air and said, "That's it. I'm not supposed to go. There are too many roadblocks, too many things getting in between me and this meeting."

And then I saw a licence plate on a car a few metres ahead. I asked the driver to move closer so I could take a picture of it with my phone.

I still have that picture on my phone.

The licence plate said, "FAITH."

It was a reminder, right when I needed it, to continue moving forward, to find a way to overcome the roadblocks so that I could attend a meeting that I knew was connected to my dream and would move me closer to it.

As you're listening to your heart and chasing the dreams of your true self, realize that change will not always come easily. There will be hooks and setbacks that try to make you feel fear or shame and make you want to revert to your false self. There will be interference and hurdles that make you say, "How can I be having so many problems while I'm doing what I know is right?"

In those moments you'll need to ask yourself, Am I going to stick on this path that I know is right, or am I going to let this little interference unsettle me to the point where I get off the path I'm supposed to be on?

The purpose of the interference is to increase your perseverance and faith.

What is faith?

> It's a belief in the unseen.
>
> It's a belief in all that you can become in all areas of your life.
>
> It says, "You got through something like this before; you can do it again."
>
> Faith is peaceful; if you can stay in a state of peace rather than filled with panic and anxiety, you can process what's going on and why you're experiencing the interference.
>
> Faith is about having awareness; when you shine a light of awareness on the interference, you can better understand what the interference is and how it is keeping you from listening to your heart.
>
> Faith is about accountability; by taking an account of your abilities, you will see that you're fully equipped to deal with the interference.

Your heart is the source of your faith and your intuition, and as such it will act as your compass. When you know you're engaging in actions that are in line with your WHO:

your heart will beat faster
you'll get those goosebumps and those shivers

there will be excitement
you'll find alignment with others who share
your dreams and your values
and the interference will be reduced

Perhaps an opportunity will come into your life in the form of someone whose dreams align with yours and you can open a bread shop together, creating less financial risk and sharing the workload so you have less time away from family. By following your heart, you can have faith that you will find an alignment that supports your dream and settles your partner's fear.

It may sound far-fetched, but it happened for us in our company. When we identified our core values and started reflecting them in everything we did, other companies that aligned with those values wanted to work with us, our happiness increased, and our growth skyrocketed.

Finding alignment between your core values and your actions will bring you peace. Practice seeking your heart's knowledge and wisdom through all the stages, by stopping before you act and asking your heart,

"Does this feel peaceful?"

When you're at a fork in the road or at a point of conflict with someone that you can't seem to move past, the right decision is what feels peaceful in your heart. That won't mean it's always peaceful through the decision, but you'll have an intuition about the peace waiting on the other side.

Have faith in that intuition.

We often talk about intuition like it's something that only women have. But really, it's an internal compass we all have — an internal voice, that gut feeling that says, "That's not quite right" or, "I feel a connection with this person" or, "I feel like I'm supposed to do this."

As you travel inward, that voice becomes stronger and becomes one you can rely on and have faith in when it says, "stay off this path" or, "go this way."

Intuition is really just about listening to your heart and following it. People often use the phrase "follow your heart" loosely, as though it's something to turn to once in a while. I believe you can embrace it more deeply than that and ALWAYS rely on your heart. If you get off the path and things aren't feeling right, it's your heart that will tell you whether your actions are in line with your values, and it will give you faith to push through barriers that stop you from living your purpose, but in a peaceful, loving, heart-centred way.

Living inward and listening to your heart is about breaking the thoughts that are attached to the hooks trying to pull you back.

The false ego will try to stop you. It will say, "Why are you doing that? Who are you to think you're capable of achieving that?"

Fear will try to stop you. It will say, "You tried that before and it didn't go very well."

Now you'll feel shame or guilt remembering something you did before.

No.

There's no shame.

That's just a distraction — a memory that no longer serves you, a memory to forgive and release and heal from.

The moment you realize that ego and fear are trying to distract you from a certain path is the moment you realize that the path exists because your heart placed it there.

Don't forget that ego is just your false self, a mask trying to pull you back to that place you lived in for so long that wasn't you.

And remember that fear is a liar trying to keep you from growth and potential and true purpose.

Remember that the journey down your heart's path is not about worrying where you're going or the exact action you're supposed to be taking. It's about understanding that as you follow your heart, you're shedding a series of lies that have grown up around you, that fear and ego put there as masks and adaptations you adopted through actions that were not aligned with your heart. These actions caused you to become confused, stressed, anxious, depressed, and fearful of, or indifferent to, your future. You came to the point of asking yourself, "How did I end up going so wrong?"

As you are shedding the masks, you're learning to listen to your heart and move towards alignment with your heart centre. As you move inward and explore the values of your heart, your mind will align with peace, gratitude, and love, while your actions will be informed by your truest nature.

As you act out your WHO in everything, it will become easier and easier to do. It will feel like you should have always been doing it because you're simply remembering and knowing who you are by shedding what is false. You'll realize that the little things you did or said in your past that you think are bad or that you're not happy with were just part of ego's process to keep you from getting to your heart centre and living your life as a soul expression of your true self.

And unquestionably, if your ego was working that hard to distract you, it's because your heart was speaking to you. For profound transformation and enlightenment in your life, you must listen to your heart.

Consulting your heart every day, finding what is peaceful,

walking down the path boldly, knowing that your heart placed this path before you for a reason, consulting your mantra and core values to know what your actions and reactions should be, are choices you get to make every day.

Small practices will add up and it will start to flow more naturally, as you believe more in who you are and in what's developing inside of you.

Celebrate this belief.

Take your authority every day because this is your life.

Rely on your strength and wisdom, because it won't always be easy, but it will always be worth it.

PRACTICE: Be the Hero

Background

Arizona was a place of retreat for me, a place to pause and refresh so that I could come back and put energy back into my workplace, my public speaking, and my mentoring of other businesses. But in pausing and embracing a growth mindset, and investing in self-care and nourishment, I realized that living inward is about discovering identity, discovering purpose, and then being the hero of your own journey by living out what you've found in every area of your life.

We all know stories of people who discover their purpose very early on; they find a talent and love of a sport, or acting, or politics, and they completely throw themselves into it because it feels so very purposeful to them and it fulfills them on a deep level because it's in alignment with their WHO. But years later, they wake up anxious, depressed, and disconnected from the very identity that used to bring them so much joy.

If I had come back from Arizona and thrown myself back into being all about workplace culture and showing love to the people I work with, I would have come to the same place I was when in I went to Arizona and eventually back to where I was at the start of this book — feeling burned out, disconnected, and as though I was busy for the sake of busyness because all my focus would have been in living my purpose and my WHO in only one area of my life: my work.

For me to feel wholly fulfilled, I needed to address every aspect of my life and examine it to ensure that I was being the authentic me in every relationship, in every activity.

Being the hero of your life means seeking balance and authenticity in every area of your life.

Being the hero of your own life is about taking an honest look at your life and asking yourself, "In what areas of my life am I failing to live authentically?"

What aspect of your life needs you to be a hero?

You may have started with your career, knowing that you're

feeling unfulfilled in it and that it's not bringing you joy and a sense of purpose. But now you're baking bread and starting to address that. So, what's next?

Because it's not enough to discover your WHO and chase your dreams in only one area of your life. You may start off feeling that you're finally reaching your potential, but if you're only doing that in one area, that will lead to unbalance, overextending yourself, and eventually being burned out and just as disconnected as you were when you started.

The Practice

This is the first part of a three-part practice that we'll cover in the remaining chapters of this book. During this part, read the questions below and journal about the answers that come to you while you think about what it looks like for you to be the hero in all aspects of your life.

Mentally visit each area of your life.

Are you authentically you with your kids?

> What kind of relationship do you want with them?
>
> Do the interactions you have with them reflect your values?

What about your relationship with your partner?

Parents, brothers, sisters?

Who do you need to forgive and experience healing with?

What kind of relationship do you want to have with yourself?

> Do you honour yourself in the way you choose to spend your free time?
> Do you honour your values in the way you spend money, or in your hobbies, or in the way you look after yourself?

Are you feeling that you're not authentic in your friendships?

> What kind of friend were you in your childhood?
> What kind of friend do you want to be or want to have?
> What kind of friend are you now?

Maybe you'll think of your best friend, and how you haven't seen her in a long time, and you have a dream to go on vacation with her. Call her and tell her how important she is to you. Let her know that even all these years later, with your lives being so busy and not having a lot of quality time together, she's still so important to you and you want to go away for a weekend and catch up.

This is what is looks like to expand your heart centre in a healthy way throughout your whole life. To be the hero.

Consult your heart to determine which area of your life needs you the most. Ask yourself what it would look like for you to have:

An authentic career

Authentic friendships

Authentic relationships with family

Authentic love and care for yourself

In what area of your life are you experiencing the most anxiety, depression, and stress?

Could this be an area where you are not living authentically?

Is your WHO coming through in your intention in the different aspects of your life

At work?

With your partner?

With your kids?

In how you speak with family and friends and people in your life?

Be the hero of your own life by "baking bread" in all aspects of your life, and have faith that the WHO you have found can be accepted and fulfilled in everything you do.

Being the hero of your own journey is about picking up what you have learned about yourself and letting it cascade out of your heart. It will take some time for it to soak into everything. It will take time for you to sort through the areas of your life that aren't reflecting your true self.

And in the areas where it doesn't, be the hero of your own life by picking up those pieces and doing what needs to be done. Enjoy the process, because you'll smile more, have joy in your heart, and feel more peace, contentment, and empowerment.

You'll feel strength and independence as you express yourself in your own authentic way, standing true to yourself, expressing care for others and for yourself, allowing yourself to be guided daily by your heart and the dreams, values, and mantra you've found there.

STAGE IV
LIVE YOUR
WHO

CHAPTER 9: BREAKING THROUGH WITH A LIGHTER TOUCH

Break Through

Every step you take on the living inward journey carries an old form of judgement with it — judgement from self and fear of judgement from others, and judgement that holds you back from your innermost potential.

This "holding back" is a trap. It is any thought you entertain that creates a gap between who you are and how you act — a gap between you and the life of your dreams, the life where you are living your WHO in everything you do and with everyone you're with.

Breaking through is about releasing your mind from the traps. The traps are created in the way we think, the way we act, the way we try to control things, and in how tightly we hold onto things.

How we touch things in life, how strongly we hold onto them as opposed to how lightly we touch them can dictate whether we feel misery or peace and joy. The lighter touch allows us to not be so strongly attached to things and it puts less pressure on us and on those around us, and in the way in which we go about chasing our dreams.

Don't mistake a lighter touch for indifference. We can still care deeply about our dreams and live our purpose, while loving others freely and authentically, giving them the freedom to be themselves.

A few years ago, I was out walking my dog, Sam. It was a frigid winter day, and the streets were empty and silent as I walked up one and down another, heading towards the river and my ten-minute spot.

I reached the end of a street and saw a woman in her driveway, packing boxes into the back of her car. Besides Sam and myself, she was the only other living creature out and about on this freezing cold day, and I had a feeling she wasn't outside by choice.

I thought about minding my own business, walking past without saying hi, but I felt a push to reach out from a place of kindness.

I walked over to her and said, "Boxes? On such a cold day? Are you moving?"

She nodded and then started to weep a little as she told me she'd lost her husband and had to leave the home she'd been in for thirty-six years. She talked about how much she loved nature and how much she was going to miss being near the water and all the birds.

I felt an instant connection with her, her love of nature and birds, and then, as if on cue, a huge bird caught my eye and I looked up. "Whoa, that's a big hawk."

She followed my gaze. "That's not a hawk. Do you see the plumage coming out of its chest? That's a baby bald eagle."

I'd heard about bald eagles being in the area, but I'd never seen one. We watched it, mesmerized, as it flew past. Just as we were about to look away, the mother eagle appeared right behind the baby. It was gorgeous, massive, with a full white head, keeping close enough to the baby to have its eye on it but far enough away to let it have space to learn.

It was a beautiful lesson for me on how to live my life with a lighter touch.

At the time, it spoke to me directly about how I should be as a parent, a husband, a friend — how to always be there if people close to me need me, but also allow them their space to explore, to lead, to go in their own direction, to be free, knowing that at any time, they can turn around and I will always be there.

Since then, the lesson of the mother eagle has returned to me many times, to remind me that I can love people and not always have to act on that love or try to hold onto the relationship too tightly. The breakthrough has come in seeing the tremendous growth I've had in my own perception of my relationships, whether longstanding or more recent.

The mother eagle is also a lesson in how we can chase our dreams with a lighter touch.

> We keep an eye on them
> We follow them
> We let them lead us
> Without trying to control them

Every word in this book is a lighter touch.

This book was my dream. When I started it, I didn't have everything planned out or know exactly what it was all going to look like. I freed that dream and shared it with people in my life who I wanted to have come along with me on this ride. But in expressing my dream, I expressed myself with a lighter touch, without a need to control the entire process or drag people along who didn't want to come with me. I expressed it and I freed it. And those who joined me on this journey did so because they have their own dreams that they can see coming true. Collectively, we're all dreaming together and moving forward with a lighter touch.

And now I'm about to release this dream to the world. As you read this, imagine me sitting in my car near the river, at my ten-minute spot. This November, my book will be self-published, and fear is definitely sitting in my passenger seat.

I have chosen to go for it all in every aspect of my life. I have written this book from my heart to reach your heart, because I believe that sharing this message is in line with my purpose. It makes me feel like I'm fully coming alive with the sensation of realizing my full potential while maintaining humility and gratitude. It is so empowering and so fulfilling.

And I want this for you. My journey is yours. Your journey is mine.

I sit here knowing that I will never be the same and I will never turn my back on what I now know is my potential. My potential is to help others to discover the same potential in themselves. To break the traps and close the gaps to the life that can only be found inside of you.

Remember, I believe your purpose is the same as mine:

> It's to discover who you are and to just be that.
>
> It's to unleash your potential in your own most unique ways.
>
> No matter what that looks like, it's yours from your heart.

Breaking through is about chasing your dreams to release your potential and close the gaps in your life with a lighter touch. And because that comes about by just being who you've discovered yourself to be, it takes the pressure off. There's not so much intense pressure about what you're trying to create, or what you have to be, or who you're with.

> You're free because you don't have to control every thing.
>
> You're free because you can offer love authentically and you can express your dreams without needing to manage the entire process.
>
> You're free to express your dreams while always going back to your heart to remember what you've learned and then move forward.

Now that you know who you are, you can break through the traps to release your dreams and commit to them with a lighter touch.

The pressure's off. Just be you.

Forgiveness with a Lighter Touch

In Chapter 5, I wrote about forgiveness as releasing all hope of a better past. This literally frees us from the past and allows us to embark on releasing our full potential. This type of forgiveness allows us the freedom and permission to discover who we are. It removes all the masks that we think we need, and it allows us to view ourselves completely differently.

But forgiveness isn't just about releasing the past. Forgiveness is also part of the present, and it's found in how we release grievances by having a lighter touch.

Grievances create traps and gaps, and forgiveness is what frees us from the traps and closes the gaps.

When we say we forgive someone, we think we're choosing to release them from some form of obligation to us. But I don't think people realize or pay attention to the incredible power and freedom that resides within the act of forgiveness, not just for the person they're forgiving, but for themselves.

We tend to think of forgiveness as being necessary for big events, big hurts, big visible actions that caused scars and masks to grow. But forgiveness is more often needed for the quiet, unseen, unspoken accumulation of grievances that add up — the grudges we hold onto, way beyond when we think we do. Even with little things — perhaps even more with little things.

> Why does my co-worker never refill the coffee pot after taking the last cup?
>
> Why do my kids always leave the cap off the tooth paste?
>
> Why does my partner leave crumbs on the counter?
>
> Why does my roommate leave laundry on the floor?

We see these little scenarios as irritations that we have to put up with.

But they're actually grievances that we need to forgive in that moment and smile at, instead. If that person was suddenly gone, would we miss them and even their crumbs? Would we want them back so we can smile at them, instead of grumble?

We have grievances with people we love, people we like, people we're not so fond of, people we don't know, and even ourselves.

> Why does my son's soccer coach always yell at the kids like that?
>
> Why did this driver just pull out in front of me?
>
> I can't believe I just did that again.

We hold minor grievances against others, and these grievances are the source of our ruminating minds. They keep coming up, day after day.

> My partner left crumbs on the counter.
>
> They did it again.
>
> I don't believe this. Crumbs. Again!

And after enough time of ruminating, day after day, on these grievances, our minds become distorted. We begin to see people differently, even people we love. It completely changes the way we see them and the way we love them and the reasons why we want to be with them.

These micro-grievances are traps. They are subtle lies about others that you accumulate and carry around without really knowing it. The heaviness of them puts you in a weakened state as you get caught up in the lies about this person and how you view them.

And then the tiny grievances add up to false beliefs that weigh you down and pull you out of peace.

> Why does my partner not talk to me the way they used to or want to spend time with me the way they used to?
>
> And why does this person who I love bother me so much?
>
> I don't enjoy being with them like I used to. Do I even love them anymore?

When we're walking through life, carrying around ten or twenty or thirty grievances, that's a lot of weight. That's a lot of distortion of our minds, and it increases the gap between who we are and how we act and how we love.

Forgiveness is what lifts the weight of these little specks of grievances that we're holding against ourselves and each other. Try to raise up those micro-grievances to a level of awareness where you can recognize them and say, "I never realized it before, but I'm having all this inner dialogue about this person and I'm holding on to all these thoughts against them."

If there's something your mind is ruminating on and that you're talking to yourself about, it's time to bring it to the surface and choose what to do about it. If it's something serious enough to speak to the person about, don't just keep it in your mind — discuss it with that person, with love and vulnerability. If it's something you bring to the surface and realize, "That's a ridiculous thing to talk to this person about," then you can let it go.

Either it's serious enough to discuss, or it's minor enough to release. But no way should you be holding onto all those tiny grievances in your head and allowing them to weigh you down and hold you back.

The forgiveness of these tiny grievances will allow you to walk through life feeling light — not heavy, not viewing everyone in your life with assumptions and negativity. Forgiveness allows you to accept people in your life for who they are and meet them where they're at.

It's important to set healthy boundaries and communicate what is important to you, but you also want to make sure you're first going through this filter process. Do you really want to talk with someone about something that doesn't actually matter very much?

In the big picture, is your co-worker not refilling the coffee pot really upsetting you or is it possible that you're caught up in the distraction from who you really are?

When the inner dialogue in your head is, "This thing really bothers me, but it doesn't bother the person next to me. Why does it irritate me so much?", ask yourself, "What can I potentially learn about this experience?"

Is it possible you're not paying attention to all the little grievances that your mind is ruminating on before you even got to work?

The toothpaste cap, the crumbs on the counter, the driver who cut you off — these micro-grievances grow to enormous size in our head. We're driving in the car saying, "I can't believe they did that. Why do they keep doing that? Do they not know how that makes me feel? They shouldn't do it." And we spend the entire car ride thinking about something that's really just a little agitation and not an accurate reflection of how we feel about the people in our lives.

Have you ever arrived somewhere and had the passing thought, "I don't even remember the drive itself"? I know that's happened to me. But now, I try to remember to always be present and let it all go, by discussing what's necessary and releasing and forgiving what just adds weight but has no real importance.

Flushing out the grievances that are silly means you won't pollute the relationships you want, and you won't ruminate on the lies. It makes you lighter in your whole approach to life when you see these grievances as opportunities to say, "Is it really them, or is it me? Do I need to talk about this with this person, or can I let it go?" It will also make your car rides much more enjoyable.

Releasing grievances is a great practice for your one-minute spot — to look at the situation you're in and the micro-grievance you're experiencing and say, "I'm going to talk about this grievance to this person because it's important," or, "I'm letting go of this thing I'm holding onto, because this relationship means more to me than this grievance. I'm letting it go because it's too heavy to carry around and it will impact my love and care for this person by coming out in the wrong way."

In some ways it's even easier to release grievances for people you're not as fond of. Why would you hold onto grievances for those people? If there's someone you've decided you don't really like being around, why carry thoughts of them around in your head all day long? That's just extra baggage that you don't need. That's just empowering the lies against you.

Realize that not offering forgiveness is actually hurting you the most. Don't listen to the voice that convinces you to continue to be trapped. Learn to smile and laugh off the small stuff.

Remember, this is a journey about your WHO; it's about your discovery of who you are and releasing the full potential of yourself and your happiness to the world.

How can you release your full potential if you're heavy with grievance?

We must forgive. It's who we are.

Forgiveness is about being loving and the freedom that it offers. It is simultaneously a form of self-care and care for others.

The breakthrough is in living moment to moment and releasing the grievances so we can live lighter and in a loving, peaceful, calm manner.

The breakthrough is about an internal condition — an internal mindset. It is about aligning our hearts and minds and bringing peace into every situation. You'll find that everything works better in this state.

Living inward is about setting the right internal condition so that the outside life we live is being lived to its fullest potential with open eyes, open ears, an open heart, an open mind, and a happy, open smile.

PRACTICE: Mind the Gap

Background

The breakthrough comes not just in an action you take, but in the realization of who you are and that you are free to be you. The breakthrough is about knowing that you don't have to break the traps or jump a gap forcefully. You can break through with a lighter touch — with the wisdom that all you have to do is be yourself and allow others to be who they are.

You can be still and find peace and contentment in the knowledge that it's not up to you to push things forward or control everything. Instead, you can offer space and approach each area of your life with a lighter touch.

The lighter touch is about approaching the traps and gaps with freedom from needing to control, and with forgiveness of grievances, so that you can mind the gaps and close them.

In Chapter 8, I wrote about being the hero in every area of life. I talk a lot about career in this book, and in the changes I've made in my working life — from leading a company, to mentoring, to public speaking, and now to writing a book. I've used career as an example of the living inward life because so many people feel disconnected and disengaged in their working life; this is usually where people first see the gap between who they are and the life they want to live.

But as I pointed out in that chapter, you need to go through this living inward process in every area of your life. The breakthrough comes not just in knowing the dreams you have for your work, your relationships, and your self-care and nourishment, but also in the realization that you did it and that you can continue to do it, but not by grabbing hold and clinging tightly.

The lighter touch allows you to be more at peace, because when you mix knowing who you are with a lighter touch, it's much easier to forgive yourself and others and much easier to experience joy in the moment because you're not thinking, *I have to make this thing perfect for a year from now.* Instead, you can say, "I'm right here and fully me in this present moment and that's all I've got."

That's where all the weight is instantly lifted, freeing both your heart and your mind.

That's a lighter touch.

The Practice

It's time to know all the traps and close the gaps. In the first part of today's practice, write out your grievances. Start with the people you love and adore. Write out the micro-grievances that you're carrying around.

Decide which of them you actually need to talk to people about; circle those ones and think about how you can address them with a lighter touch, with love, humility, and vulnerability. Think about how you can express your grievance while remaining true to yourself and honouring the other person, allowing both of you the freedom to be who you are.

For the remaining items, which you've decided are too minor to talk about but too heavy to carry around, cross them off the list one at a time. As you cross each one off, say outloud, "I will honour this person and myself in the way that I respond to this situation. In the future, when this grievance comes up, my inner dialogue will not be one of lies, but of saying, 'Stop. That thought does not honour who I am or the relationship I want to have with this person.' I release this grievance so that I no longer have to carry it around. In fact, I have learned to smile at it because of acceptance."

Once you've completed this exercise for the people you love, repeat it for the people you like, and then for the people you are less fond of. Work your way through the minor grievances you have day to day, and commit to moving forward, free of the weight of these grievances, and with a mindset to approach life with a lighter touch.

The second part of this practice is to identity traps in your life and plan for your dream life by setting goals, so that over time you close the gaps. It's time to take stock of who you are and the life you wish to live. It's time to get ready to free your dreams and commit to the best version of your life that is guided by your heart.

Look back at your work in the practice in Chapter 8, where you identified different areas of your life in which you wanted more of your WHO to shine through.

Think about your life and those areas you identified as if they are slices of a pie.

> How many slices are there and what are they called?
>
> Maybe one is marriage and you label it with the name of your partner.
>
> One each for your kids.
>
> One for your career and the title of your job.
>
> One for self-nourishment and care and what you do to honour yourself.
>
> One for faith and belief.

Use the following chart to give each one a name. When filling in the pie chart, think about these aspects as growth opportunities to have every single one of them be healthy and fully connected to your best self.

After filling out as many slices as pertain to your life, ask yourself the following questions for each slice, and write down beside each slice what comes to mind:

> What about this aspect of my life am I not content with?
>
> What relationships are being hindered by grievances or need deeper forgiveness?

> Who am I judging?
>
> What failure did I have in this area that I am not letting go of?

Go through each, and journal about what you find. Then ask yourself:

> Do these thoughts still serve me?
>
> Do they help me or hinder me?
>
> Do they empower me and others, or contaminate my relationships?
>
> Am I feeling encouraged or deflated?

In answering those questions, you've started to identify the traps for each piece of the pie.

This is where the breakthrough happens. Right here. This is where you truly learn to be the hero of your life and commit to the life you want. This is where you see the dreams you have for every area of your life and get ready to free them and commit to them.

But first, you must experience a breakthrough as you say goodbye to the lies and the traps that are keeping you from who you are. Imagine each individual trap that you identified — the traps that are holding you back from being your best and truest self in all areas of your life. Imagine them sitting in the palm of your hand, and then let each one fly away.

Look for a sense of peace to wash over you as you let each one of them go, saying, "This does not serve me anymore. I love myself enough to be whole, to be who I am at my core, and to reach my full potential."

Your goal is no more traps. It's time to let yourself be free.

DISCOVER YOUR WHO LIFE CHART

Example chart: This person is on their journey to discovering their WHO and is seeking to align their outward actions in each area of their life with what they are discovering inside.

Start your own Discover Your Who Life chart below by looking into your own heart to identify the important slices of your life. You may have areas that are over- or under-developed; discovering your WHO is about creating a healthy balance so that your heart can drive what's important to you at the identity level in ALL facets of life. With this chart you are creating your way of living, no longer with random actions and reactions. You are going to love yourself enough to live from your heart-centre.

CHAPTER 10: FREE YOUR DREAMS AND COMMIT

Tell Everyone and Take Action

After the offsite, we decided to hold a company-wide celebration like never before, with the intention of releasing our identity and new culture to the entire organization. I didn't want to announce it over an email; I wanted everyone to have the opportunity to feel the excitement and the emotions attached to such a transformative change.

A tremendous amount of work went into the internal launch. I formed a small crew and they worked tirelessly, with incredible care and commitment for everyone in the company. Planning the event turned into a mission that filled early mornings and long days, and as we saw it coming together, we knew we were building something special. We arranged for speakers to talk about happiness and wellness, and planned other activities, with the hope of providing increased understanding and connectivity across the company. We had every detail planned, with lots of surprises scheduled throughout the day, all of it leading towards the unveiling and explanation of our personality and culture as a renewed and transformed company.

We booked a superb event location, right in the heart of our region's tech community. I watched everyone arriving on that beautiful sunny morning, seeing the smiles and looks of surprise as they were welcomed by a steel drum band and were handed a healthy smoothie to start their day.

Everyone mingled and explored the room, with six giant screens displaying our happy face logo and our soon-to-be announced mantra, I'M IN. The sun filled the windows, the steel drum music filled the air, and laughter and smiles filled our faces; already it was feeling like a success. At that moment, I felt more engaged in my career than ever before, watching my dream coming true of helping others to find deeper connections with each other and with our company.

I took on the responsibility of MC and ensuring that key points were communicated. I had never spoken in front of our entire company before, and it was scary to think that the first time would be on such a radical (at least for us) topic. But in my heart, I knew this was a step I needed to take, both for my own growth and to enact systemic changes, by showing that our identity as a caring company started with the leadership revealing our identities as caring individuals.

The morning of the event, my inner dialogue and fear were having their way with me and I was a nervous wreck. But, as I walked up on stage, all the fear and doubt melted away. I felt more whole, more purposeful, and more myself, as if not only was the message right, but so was standing in front of an audience and delivering it. My fear of not being able to speak publicly was gone, and I experienced a total flow state, feeling complete in each moment. It was my first full view of my seeds of purpose that led me to where I am now. It was a moment that gripped me in a feeling that I didn't want to ever have leave my mind or body or heart.

We launched I'M IN and explained why it was to become our mantra. Then out came our company purpose and explanation of how it aligned with what matters most to us. Finally, we shared our values and our desire to create a safe, happy environment, where mind, body, and spirit could all be nurtured.

Staff were invited up to receive their I'M IN T-shirt and take a break, with coffee, pastries, and fruit.

As our public speakers came up and the day progressed, I could see what it meant for people to feel excited, purposeful, and whole. I knew transformation was occurring even beyond this room; I had dreams of how reducing stress and increasing happiness for our employees would benefit their families, with employees possibly taking joy home with them at the end of each workday.

At the end of the event, we all went back to the office for an outdoor lunch and more surprises for our staff. We had painted the walls with chalkboard paint, and the I'M IN crew had created culture art over the walls of the office and the kitchen, reminding us all of who we are and where we're going. On everyone's desk was a brand-new culture card, detailing our mantra, purpose, and values, and I had signed a declaration on the back of each card, binding myself to be IN with them all.

After lunch, I stood looking around the office, taking in the smiles and relaxed atmosphere. I had poured my heart into this change at a level that I didn't really understand until that moment, and I was overcome. I released a giant breath, my eyes welled up with tears, and then I completely hit the wall — I was depleted.

Leaving the festivities to continue on without me, I made my way into the boardroom. I turned off the lights, lay down under the table, and — spent and exhausted — fell asleep. When I woke up, I went home and straight to bed and slept into the next day. Upon returning to the office, it was evident that something had changed; something had broken for the good, both in the company and in me.

The launch was just the first step of unleashing our WHO. After telling everyone internally, we continued to take action and make changes that reflected our new personality as a company. We stayed focused on listening, learning, and implementing, and watched the business, and the individuals within it, completely come alive.

As an organization, we started on a path to become healthier. We offered to pay for a baseline of health to be established for all of our employees from a naturopathic doctor, and over a third of our staff jumped at the chance. We implemented yoga classes, invested in exercise areas and equipment, hired a personal trainer, and ended up winning an international award for being one of the healthiest organizations in the world. We dropped stringent dress codes and adopted flexible hours; everyone was given the freedom to take breaks and go for walks around the lake on our property at any time of any day.

We continued to have authentic talks and dialogues. We embraced gratitude, empathy, resiliency, forgiveness, hope, and ways to show compassion and care for each other and ourselves. We welcomed children on any day to our office, because we identified family as being important to us as a company. We allowed staff to bring their dogs to work and hang out with their owners and other staff. This all added up to a reduction in stress and a calmness that began to permeate through the entire building.

While all this was transpiring, record sales were happening and, by all accounts, all of our major key performance indicators were improving. Looking back to our offsite a few months earlier, I almost couldn't believe that we had come so far just from asking the question "Who Am I?" of our business. The power of WHO had allowed us to discover and release the very personality of our business, both internally and externally. In every decision we made and action we took from then on, our WHO was at the core. From there, a gravitational pull occurred, creating staggering results that we had never seen before in recruitment, sales, and strategic relationships.

It was working beyond my wildest dreams!

In business, change often needs to be accompanied by a public announcement; otherwise, it will be confusing for your staff and your customers. Our company-wide celebration was the start of telling everyone internally, after which we began telling the world by putting our mantra and purpose on all of our external marketing, such as our website and business cards.

Because so much of my personal journey was happening alongside the business changes, the external launch of the authentic me coincided with our company-wide celebration. But naturally not everyone in my life was at that launch, and from time to time I still come across people I knew from before who never had the chance to meet the real me.

Several months ago a friend of mine, who I hadn't seen in several years, contacted me. He wanted me to meet and do business with someone, so we set up a meeting. During the meeting my friend sat in silence. I had gone through profound changes — some might say a total rebirth — since last seeing him. I knew a lot of the changes I'd experienced were coming out naturally during the meeting, and in passing I wondered what he thought.

He left the meeting that day shaking my hand and thanking me. Shortly afterwards, I received a beautiful note that would've been completely out of character from the man that I knew before. He asked to get together for lunch, because he felt inspired and wanted to get to know me again. We met for lunch and we sat and talked for hours. It was amazing, and I learned things that were important to him that we never would have talked about before.

This is what happens when you enter a stage of freeing your dreams, committing to them, and releasing who you've found yourself to be to everyone. It's not always about making a big announcement; it just means living out your authentic self for others to see and to know who you truly are.

Once you have expressed your authentic self in all aspects of your life to people who matter, your authentic self will start to flow out naturally in everything that you do.

You'll know when it's time to show the true expression of yourself and communicate authentically, because you won't be able to stop your true self from flowing out.

When you take this step, be prepared for a transformation of your relationships. Your changes will elicit responses in people that you can't always predict. For myself, the changes in me were so profound, and they informed actions that were so different from before, that I'm sure some people weren't sure how to react. I went from being a lone wolf to all of a sudden wanting to visibly lead our company. People who had been part of our company for a long time thought they knew me, or a version of me, and when this version arose, there was certainly a lot of eyebrow-raising.

Living who you are doesn't mean that everyone is going to move forward with you and that every relationship is going to be perfect. People will respond to you in their own way. Friends might say, "I haven't seen this side of you before. I don't know how to relate to this." Some people will say, "This is amazing; I love what you're doing."

Some people may pull away, and it's OK to give them room, making space for new people to come into your life who resonate with who you are now. You may realize that some of the people in your life just don't feel right to you anymore, because you don't feel that they're willing to accept your growth, and in some ways, they might be holding you back.

Is it OK for us to love some people from far away and not so close? I think so. We wish them well; we wish them love. But we love ourselves enough to soar and keep growing as our authentic selves.

If I've lost some connectivity with people who can't understand or relate to who I am, then it's not the desired connectivity that I want in my life right now. I try to live my life with loving kindness, compassion, and forgiveness, and I offer the door for anyone to enter, but I can't make anyone walk through it.

In place of some relationships that I've lost, I've gained this mountain of incredible connectivity with others. The amount of profound honesty and authenticity I have received from being honest and authentic has been overwhelmingly more valuable than what I had before. For the most part, my relationships have deepened with the people who are closest to me. I have profound friendships now that I never had before, while the truly impactful relationships I had before have deepened into something stronger and more fulfilling.

The relationship I have with my co-founder, who has known me and been my friend since I was 16, is a beautiful story. Who knew that even though we approach life philosophically and spiritually from different angles, we would still come to a place that is so similar, where we can go deep and discuss things that we never have before? And how exciting that it affects the way we look at the world and how we can impact it, and our company, differently.

The people in your life who truly love you will look to accept you.

They might not understand what these changes are or what they mean but they'll say, "Let me get to know who this authentic version of you is. Let me encourage you on this new path you're on."

If someone can't encourage you, ask yourself, what path were they encouraging you to be on before?

Those who have problems accepting the true version of you can't help you anymore. If they can't accept you for who you really are, they are a hook back to your false self and you'll recognize how they feed the false self. You continue to love them but maybe from a distance, with a hope that they come back and with a door that's always open for them. They are on their own journey. Release them with the hope that your authentic paths will cross again.

Those who can't encourage you are the ones who were encouraging you to be on a path that reinforced their own masks. If you take off your mask, it encourages others to take off theirs. By being you, you are helping others to be themselves, but there may be those who are not yet comfortable being who they are. They may be a bit bewildered by who you are revealing yourself to be and by the fact that you are no longer reinforcing their masks.

Part of your authenticity is not just, for lack of a better word, the "exposure" of you, but the exposure of what was false in others and in how you saw yourself through their eyes. Ask yourself what they were doing for you and what you were doing for them. People can't stay in your life for the wrong reasons. It's not easy to let them go, but you can't live with the false attachments anymore.

Remember the lesson of the breakthrough: be yourself and allow others the freedom to be who they are.

The Journey Doesn't End

In telling everyone and taking action, your WHO is now leading you on this journey, and you are the hero, working towards releasing the truest version of yourself to everyone and in every area of your life.

Being the hero of your own journey is about freeing your dreams and seeing what the seeds of purpose are within those dreams and then living that purpose outwards in everything you do.

It's about believing that you can consult your heart at any time to remember who you are and that you can have faith that your heart will give you the wisdom to deal with anything that gets in the way, but in a loving, compassionate way that is authentic to you. Your actions will be driven by your values, and in a way that honours others while allowing them to see who you truly are.

Living inward is about checking in with yourself every day and choosing to be the authentic you in every aspect of your life, and choosing to live your soul expression in everything you do.

It's about consulting your imagination to see what the dream looks like for that area of your life, following your intuition and taking small steps to move towards that dream. As you move towards the dream, remember to look back and heal and offer forgiveness to yourself and others, where necessary. Remember to pause and invest in self-nourishment, when necessary. When challenges or threats or anxiety arise, are you going to react in the old way, wearing the old masks, or are you going to choose your true nature, having faith in your abilities, releasing grievances, and breaking the traps with a lighter touch? Even after discovering who you are, you still have a choice, no matter how far into this journey you are.

Being the hero is about letting go of anything that holds you back, about no longer entertaining anything that stops you from being who you are with your family, your friends, in your career, in your care for yourself, and in your interactions with everyone and everything you come in contact with.

It's about living your purpose all the time and feeling the potential in you.

You may fall back into old habits once in a while. That's OK. This isn't about pressure. It should feel soothing to be the hero of your own journey.

You know the direction you're taking now. You don't feel lost anymore.

You're using your ten-minute spot to remember who you are — to go back to the foundation of your heart — and you're using the one-minute spot to be led by your heart and to release grievances in any moment.

You have a hope and a strategy for your life, and you know what to do that will make life even more fulfilling. It's a very hopeful state to be in and you'll see how you can achieve it in every area of life.

It doesn't mean everything will flow easily. But things will make sense, and you'll have realizations and truer relationships. You'll want to nourish and grow what you've found in your heart.

You won't want to deviate or make concessions. (You might make concessions in your career, but definitely not in your personal life.)

As the hero of your journey, you're going to uphold what you've found in your heart and not get caught up in distractions or entertain toxic thoughts.

So many of us attach our dreams to other people. We look at them and say, "Why them and not me?" The hero lets those thoughts go. You were made to live out your own journey, a journey as unique as your own fingerprint. You can't control the future; all you can do is try your best to be the hero of your authentic self within each moment that you have and repeat it every day, gaining a conscious awareness to remember who you are and truly enjoy your beautiful journey.

For me, the journey to remember who I am has led me to know that I am a man who loves people and who wants everyone to find their purpose and find deep fulfillment in their lives. Plain and simple. It's what was revealed within my awakening when I shone a light of awareness on my identity. And when I get scared to express that aspect of who I am, I find my life slows down until I remember again. Then once I remember, I am reminded that thoughts need actions. I am at my purest identity when I not only remember who I am but also choose to act on that wisdom in every area of my life. I am at my best when I am fully me and I weave love and care as the thread into everything I do. I am at my best when

I remember my true identity — that I am a man who talks about love.

Why do we find it so hard to speak of love? We get embarrassed that we need and want love more than anything else in our lives because it makes us feel weak and vulnerable to admit it. But isn't that in itself the biggest lie if indeed it's what we all want the most?

When we're born, full of dreams and full of purpose, we open our eyes and look around for love that comes to us in the form of a soft caress, a warm look, or a playful tickle.

At the end of our lives, we hope that we experienced love fully and truly, that we gave it freely, and received it graciously.

All those years later, even though so much has changed, our desire to experience love remains the same.

But so often, we get lost in the middle of our lives without it, feeling that disconnection and failing to express love either to ourselves or those around us, failing to give and receive love in ways that are authentic to who we are.

To me, the journey of living inward is all about love. It's about loving your true self enough to go on a journey to remember yourself, to find yourself, to take the mask off and uncover yourself.

It's about loving yourself enough to remember dreams of youth, discover current dreams, and then pursue those dreams, but in a way that displays love to those around you and honours and respects everyone you come in contact with.

The living inward journey is like travelling through a tunnel — your focus is on the light at the end, it's on what you hope to find at the end of the tunnel. You hope to find your true self waiting for you with a life of joy and purpose and fulfillment. You hope that at the end of the tunnel, you'll discover who you truly are, you'll enjoy more authentic dialogue, and you'll live from your heart.

As you move more through this process of knowing who you are — as you move through the tunnel, shedding the false self and aligning more and more with who you are and living more and more the life you were born to live — I believe you'll find that the light at the end of the tunnel is love.

> The end of the tunnel is love.
>
> Your true identity is love.
>
> Discover your WHO? Your WHO is love.

Reaching the end of this book doesn't mean you have reached the end of your journey. Doors will continue to open to you. Be open to these doors just as they are open to you.

Profound, unexpected beauty for your life is waiting with the door wide open, and all you need is the courage to walk through. Leave the fear behind you just like the steps you took to get here.

Small are the steps — there is no need for big ones. Just open your eyes and keep looking around you while you continue to look inside.

Inside of you lies the life you have always known deep down could be possible.

A life where aloneness fades, and the scars of our lives smooth over to reveal a forgiveness and compassion not only for others but for ourselves.

A life that was meant to be.

A life of smiles, joy, and abundance within ourselves.

A life of never again feeling alone but a love for oneself and others and a deep knowing and realization beyond hope that this life we live can be, should be, and is indeed more.

Inside each of us lies the door that opens up to the real truth we have always known: that our deepest desire and purpose to express our authentic self can be realized and fully accepted, and that living your WHO will lead to a life of peace, joy, potential, and boundless and transformative love.

PRACTICE: The Commit

Remember the pie chart you completed in Chapter 9? This is now the time to set yourself up for your journey ahead and commit to the kind of life you wish to have.

Remember what it was like when someone asked you as a kid, "What do you want to be when you grow up?"

Now I'm asking you again. Picture the life that you want.

> What are the slices called?
>
> What does each slice include?

Using the chart, for each aspect, fill in what your life will look like in one year.

You can set any wish and want here — even add new slices that aren't currently in your life.

> How loving will you be in your relationship with your children?
>
> What kind of career will you have?
>
> Will you be biking five times a week?
>
> Have graduated?

Got married?

Had children?

Will you have you read 25 books?

Found your faith?

Set these intentions; be intentional about the life you wish to have.

Where will you live?

Will you have new friends?

Don't hold back! Get in touch with your inner child and let your dreams unfold before your very eyes.

Now, look back at the chart you did in the last practice and compare it with this new chart.

What you have created is the hero's gap: your current state versus your future state.

It's time to close the gaps and set goals to keep yourself connected daily to your intentions so that you can free your dreams, commit to them, and make them your reality.

Don't feel bound by the timing of it. You've set your intentions on one year from now, but more important than timing is the realization of your WHO and the fact that you are becoming more of yourself in your outward actions every day.

More and more, you will see your mind aligning with your heart. Your mind is incredibly powerful, and once you decide this is where you're going, your heart will keep your mind motivated and purposeful.

You've now identified the journey and it's time to set some goals. It's time to take these intentions that you have written down and that you've said, "I want and will have."

To make your intentions real, write a commitment letter from yourself to yourself — a commitment letter to mind the gap, to pay attention, to see where you need to break through with a lighter touch, to be aware of what you're holding onto too tightly, and to know where you need to express your dreams and free them to become reality.

Write down your goals on a separate piece of paper and carry them with you wherever you go.

Every morning, use a one-minute spot to state your goals out loud and imagine them coming true and getting closer and closer to being real. Read the commitment letter you wrote to yourself, and then go forward in your day, living in the present moment, closing the gap, making it smaller and smaller, getting closer and closer to living the life that's in your heart.

Enjoy the sense of expectancy.

This is now your journey, and you are your own hero, with clarity of your mission ahead, living inward with every moment so that you can continue to close the gap and break through to YOU.

Remember: The path is you, and you are the path.

I wish you much love.

DISCOVER YOUR WHO LIFE CHART

For each area in your life, set a goal to get started. The purpose is to be exploratory in each area, to look into your heart and find a goal that will push each slice of your life forward as an expression of who you are. Then commit to each slice with an action that comes from your heart-centre.

For example, in the "Kids" slice of the sample chart, this person has gone into their heart and imagined the relationship they want with their son and then set a goal to move towards that dream. The Discover Your Who Life chart is a living document. Come back to it frequently to remember what matters to you, to remind yourself of your goals, and to set new ones as your heart directs.

ENDNOTES

Chapter 2

"culture eats strategy for breakfast"

Moore, B., and Rose, J. (2000). Recovered paper trading: Ready for the Web? *PIMA's North American Papermaker: The Official Publication of the Paper Industry Management Association, 82*(9), 28.

Chapter 4

"Why aren't you President?"

I did enjoy the role of president of our company for a time, but I reached a point of recognizing that there were others who could fill this role better than I could. Again, ego and agenda in my own life had to be set aside for the good of our company. I had other dreams I wanted to pursue, and the dream of president was not mine. Part of leadership is recognizing which roles within the organization are best suited to you and stepping aside when necessary, so you don't hold yourself back or your company.

Chapter 6

"60% of millennials are open to a different job opportunity"
Adkins, A. (2016). Millennials: The Job-Hopping Generation. *Gallup.* https://www.gallup.com/workplace/236474/millennials-job-hopping-generation.aspx

I'm John, Identity Author, Speaker, and Transformation Specialist. I speak and teach about the importance and power of knowing and loving who you are, and what you do in this world. I help businesses and "heroes in the making" uncover that their purpose is to discover their natural identity. By looking and living inward, individuals and companies can answer the question "Who Am I?"